"*These nineteenth- and early-twentieth-century
biographies, now republished by Chelsea House,
reveal an unsuspected significance. Not only are a
good many of them substantively valuable (and by
no means entirely superseded), but they also evoke
a sense of the period, an intimacy with the
attitudes and assumptions of their times.*"
—*Professor Daniel Aaron*

FRANKLIN IN PARIS.

Other titles in this Chelsea House series:

BENJAMIN FRANKLIN
JOHN BACH McMASTER

INTRODUCTION BY
LARZER ZIFF

American Men and Women of Letters Series

GENERAL EDITOR
PROFESSOR DANIEL AARON
HARVARD UNIVERSITY

CHELSEA HOUSE
NEW YORK, LONDON
1980

AAU9010

Library of Congress Cataloging in Publication Data

McMaster, John Bach, 1852-1932.
    Benjamin Franklin.

    (American men and women of letters)
    Reprint of the 1893 ed. published by Houghton,
Mifflin, Boston, under title: Benjamin Franklin as
a man of letters, which was issued in series:
American men of letters.
    Includes bibliographical references.
    1. Franklin, Benjamin, 1706-1790.   2. Authors,
American--18th century--Biography.   3. Statesmen--
United States--Biography.   I. Series.   II. Series:
American men of letters.
[PS751.M3 1980]   973.3'2'0924 [B]   80-23681
ISBN 0-87754-161-2

CONTENTS

CHAPTER I.

1706–1723.

CHAPTER II.

1723–1729.

CHAPTER III.

1729–1748.

CHAPTER IV.

1732–1748.

CHAPTER V.

1743–1756.

CHAPTER VI.

1756–1764.

CHAPTER VII.

1764–1776.

CHAPTER VIII.

1776–1790.

CHAPTER IX.

General Introduction

THE VISITABLE PAST
Daniel Aaron

THE TWENTY-FIVE BIOGRAPHIES of American worthies reissued in this Chelsea House series restore an all but forgotten chapter in the annals of American literary culture. Some of the authors of these volumes—journalists, scholars, writers, professional men—would be considered amateurs by today's standards, but they enjoyed certain advantages not open to their modern counterparts. In some cases they were blood relations or old friends of the men and women they wrote about, or at least near enough to them in time to catch the contemporary essence often missing in the more carefully researched and authoritative later studies of the same figures. Their leisurely, impressionistic accounts—sometimes as interesting for what is omitted as for what is emphasized—reveal a good deal about late Victorian assumptions, cultural and social, and about the vicissitudes of literary reputation.

Each volume in the series is introduced by a recognized scholar who was encouraged to write an idiosyncratic appraisal of the biographer and his work. The introductions vary in emphasis and point of view, for the biographies are not of equal quality, nor are the writers memorialized equally appealing. Yet a kind of consensus is discernible in these random assessments: surprise at the insights still to be found in ostensibly unscientific and old-fashioned works; in some instances admiration for the solidity and liveliness of the biographer's prose and quality of mind; respect for the pioneer historians among them who made excellent use of the limited material at their disposal.

The volumes in this American Men and Women of Letters series contain none of the startling "private" and "personal" episodes modern readers have come to expect in biography, but they illuminate what Henry James called the "visitable past." As such, they are of particular value to all students of American cultural and intellectual history.

Cambridge, Massachusetts
Spring, 1980

INTRODUCTION
TO THE
CHELSEA HOUSE EDITION
Larzer Ziff

IN MARCH 1883, D. Appleton & Co. published the first volume of what was going to be yet another multivolume history of the United States. Many were surprised. Surely the great histories of Bancroft and Hildreth had covered the ground already! To the extent they had failed to do so, specific histories of certain periods or institutions could be justified. But why begin another mammoth survey of a country that, after all, as the date 1883 signalized, was but one hundred years old in its recognized independence?

Besides, who was this John Bach McMaster? Bancroft had written from a firm center among New England literary giants such as Emerson, Longfellow, and Hawthorne, and he had brought to his work national political experience. Hildreth had written from the center of high Federalism, and he had brought to his work a wealth of personal knowledge about the great men of that influential party. But McMaster was a Princeton instructor in, of all things, civil engineering, and he had no formal training in history, was unacquainted with any great men, and was identified with neither party nor region.

The Appleton firm, which had accepted the history after its rejection by others, was all too wary of such criticism and offered a first edition of but 1,500 copies. At the same time, arrangements were made for the *Century Magazine* to serialize the opening chapters in order to soften the public's resistance to yet another trudge through the American past. But against all probabilities, the *Century* found its number disappearing from the newsstands so quickly it had to print two additional runs, and within ten days of the book's publication Appleton printed a second edition; in the following month printed a third; and in the month after yet a fourth.* McMaster's *History* had become one of the major literary events of its era and from the date of the first volume to 1913, when the eighth and final volume appeared, was eagerly read by the general public as well as by

* For publication facts and for details of McMaster's life, I have relied upon Eric F. Goldman, *John Bach McMaster* (Philadelphia, 1943).

presidents, Supreme Court justices, capitalists, and literary men, while, in a set of graded texts, it also reached millions of school children.

The title, *A History of the People of the United States,* provides a clue toward explaining the work's originality and its popularity. So convinced was McMaster that it was possible to write a history of the people rather than of the nation as a political entity that, as William T. Hutchinson observed, he almost apologized for the fact that he would also have to treat "of wars, conspiracies, and rebellions; of presidents, of congresses, of embassies, of treaties, of the ambition of political leaders in the senate-house, and of the rise of great parties in the nation." "Yet," McMaster went on to say, "the history of the people shall be the chief theme." Accordingly, the American people were for the first time presented in an account of the national past that did not center on portraits of great men. McMaster did not debunk the mythic stature of such as Washington or Jefferson, he simply ignored it in the attention he paid the daily details of their world. Dress, business pursuits, leisure occupations, changes in morals and manners, reforming movements, and technological improvements—these formed the substance of McMaster's *History.*

To an important extent, of course, McMaster pursued his theme by design. But there is also reason to believe that he did so from an outlook bred by necessity after he commenced his researches. He was, at the outset, an instructor of civil engineering untrained in history yet driven by a curiosity of awesome dimension. He was unconnected with any who could make him privy to collections of private papers or knowledgeably discuss with him the theory of history. As a result, he pursued his arduous labors by fighting to gain admittance to the libraries of historical societies, which in his day were closed rooms where documents reposed but were not read. The term *librarian* was bestowed on men who more accurately could be called wardens. One such custodian was vexed to find McMaster returning after firmly being denied admission because he had no social connection with the institution, and shocked after finally admitting McMaster to learn that he intended not only to spend the entire morning there but to return day after day for months. Nobody ever used collections in that way, even though, in this particular case, the collections happened to be those of the State of New York. What McMaster focused on in the materials available to him were the countless pamphlets, newspapers, and journals which spoke of the immediate concerns and habits of their day in a fierce sectarian spirit. Those contemporary writers viewed the leaders of the moment, whom posterity would come to venerate, as fallible if not something worse. No historian had ever traveled so far into this dense underbrush of detail, and if McMaster's *History* is open to the criticism that he frequently failed to see the forest for the trees, he was the first historian to note that the American forest was made up of a multitude of individual growths and that the trees which towered did so as much because of as despite their neighbors.

The first volume of the *History* had appeared in March, and by June McMaster was established in the new chair of American history at the University of Pennsylvania. There, he was the first professor in the United States to combine teaching with research and the writing of history, and there he remained for almost fifty years, one of the luminaries of the city Benjamin Franklin had shaped and one of the giants of the university Benjamin Franklin had founded. But when he accepted the invitation to contribute a volume on Benjamin Franklin to the American Men of Letters series, the book he produced in 1887 was no more marked by hero worship than was his *History*.

Benjamin Franklin also was to be seen in the context of the petty as well as the major struggles of his day. His writings were measured with a sharp sense of their particular context: who had already written on the same issue; what the opposition had to say; how Franklin stood to gain or lose personally as well as what his stand meant publicly.

Now, almost one hundred years after McMaster wrote his book on Franklin, a definitive edition of Franklin's writings is finally appearing. Before, the standard collection consisted of ten volumes edited by Albert H. Smyth from 1905 to 1907. But McMaster had available to him only corrupt texts, a good number of which he was the first to expose as such in his book; a muddled set of misattributions which, again, he was the first to identify as such; and a raft of unreprinted material that he dug out of neglected periodicals and pronounced to be the important literary works we have since accepted that they are—the *Dogood Papers* among them. His *Benjamin Franklin* differs from other books in the Men of Letters series because in it the writer is not only discussing a canon but establishing it. And most remarkable in this connection is the skill with which McMaster blends the two enterprises: the process of discovering unrecognized works and exposing misattributed or misinterpreted works is woven into the larger narrative of Franklin's life, which never halts or flags for such considerations. As a result, the reader experiences the pleasure of seeing a shrewd historian at work in addition to being presented with a number of judgments that even in the latter part of the twentieth century retain their power to provoke.

To McMaster's day, books about Benjamin Franklin accepted the myth of the man—the runaway apprentice who came to stand before kings; the poor boy who rose to wealth; the private citizen who shaped a city and founded a nation; the tinkering layman who made major scientific discoveries—and were principally concerned with documenting it. McMaster starts from the other end, the documents themselves, and allows Benjamin Franklin to emerge from them and to grow to whatever stature the evidence permits. He accepts the *Autobiography* as a major work of literature but not as a record of the facts—these he prefers to establish from independent sources. With his characteristic appetite for the periodical press, he is constantly aware of the relation any given work of Franklin's bears to similar works in its time and place, and thus, for example, is able to offer an incisive estimate of *Poor Richard's Almanac* in

terms of its predecessors and its competitors.
At first glance, this approach diminishes
Franklin's achievement—Poor Richard was far
from a remarkably original conception. But the
result, at second glance, is an explanation of
Franklin's real achievement—the almanac was
the same and yet much, much better for the
specific alterations that McMaster detects in
Franklin's handling. In short, McMaster returns
Franklin to history both when discussing his
writings and when discussing, as he must, a
representative range of his other activities.
After all is said and done about the remarkable
success Franklin had as a printer, just who were
the other printers of his town, what were they
printing, and how were they received? This
McMaster sets forth concisely and clearly, and
he pictures Franklin the politician and Franklin
the scientist in the same fashion.

In view of the heavy tone of veneration
Franklin had evoked from earlier historians
and biographers, McMaster's treatment could
not but have the air of iconoclasm. After re-
viewing the accomplishments of the American
printing industry in 1785, he says, "Yet for all
this activity we owe nothing to Franklin." Or
when looking at Franklin's entanglement in
local politics, McMaster observes, "In public
life Franklin displayed great executive power

mingled with traits which cannot be too strongly condemned." Or, perhaps most notoriously, he reverses expectations when he writes, "It is now the fashion to reproach him as a teacher of a candle-end saving philosophy in which morality has no place," only to continue, "The reproach, if it be one, is just." The fashion of Franklin-baiting to which McMaster referred was not to be found in histories but in imaginative literature and popular political writings. Both Thoreau and Melville before the Civil War, for example, had each in his way called into question the value to America of revering the pinch-penny ethic of Poor Richard and of encouraging the rude jostle up success's ladder exemplified by the hero of Franklin's *Autobiography*. After the war, protests against the accelerating concentration of capital in the hands of the few frequently conveyed a feeling that the Franklin myth was propagated as an example to the working man in order to reconcile him to the massive profits of the capitalist and to teach him to place the blame for his own straitened condition on himself rather than the organization of his society.

McMaster's Franklin in some ways resembles the Franklin of such dissenters. But McMaster himself was the model of a new kind of self-made man, the historian and professor

who had arrived at his eminence because of
published achievements rather than because of
privileged connections. And while he in part
shared the spirit of dissent, he had also ex-
perienced the marketplace. Thus, after scorning
Franklin's lack of morality, he goes on to say
of Franklin's policy of counseling what pays,
"Low as such a motive may seem from a moral
standpoint, it is, from a worldly standpoint,
sound and good. Every man whose life the
world calls successful has been actuated by it,
and Franklin is no exception." If, on one hand,
McMaster's Franklin was reduced to historical
realities and so differentiated from the mythic
Franklin of other biographers, on the other
hand he was so firmly grounded in human
nature as to be differentiated also from the
mechanical opportunist of the literary and political dissenters. It is this mixture of genuine
greatness and common humanity that makes
McMaster's Franklin a significant figure in the
history of American history, one that all sub-
sequent interpreters have been compelled to
confront.

In his *History*, McMaster had written that up
to 1784 "no American writer had yet appeared
whose compositions possessed more than an
ephemeral interest." But in the wake of the in-
stitutionalization of American history in which

McMaster played so prominent a part, American literature too came to be studied in detail, and one hundred and fifty years of literary composition was unearthed beneath 1784. The greatest single pioneer in this mining was Moses Coit Tyler, who, in the course of his labors, consulted with McMaster in 1893. But if McMaster's statement about 1784 was startling when he made it, it was so because he had begun American literature so early, so far before Irving and Cooper, Emerson and Hawthorne. He was asked to write on Franklin in a series devoted to American writers because the editor, Charles Dudley Warner, was intrigued by the prospect McMaster offered of pushing American literature back to so early a point.

It is clear that McMaster brought to his task the strengths of a historian rather than those of a literary critic. But in the literary area, in addition to his valuable clarifications of the Franklin canon and despite his occasional outbursts of prudish censure—all the more irritating because the reader senses that once McMaster is safely ensconced in an armchair in his men-only club he is quite willing to relish the ribald Franklin— McMaster did succeed in establishing the great printer, philanthropist, scientist, and politician as a great man of letters also. None has since disputed Franklin's title to this rank. McMaster recognized the enormous debt, beginning with literal copying and proceeding through imitation, that Franklin owed the great English prose writers of the eighteenth century, but he was the first also to recognize that a metamorphosis had taken place. Subtly but surely as Franklin's writings follow on, one witnesses the development of a simpler syntax than that of the models, a homelier and more vigorous diction, and a range of personae that is both broad and yet unified by each, be he king or farmer, heartily sharing the motives that drive the common man. Taken together these features go a long way toward defining what is American about American writing, and McMaster's noting of them is remarkable as a contribution not only to the study of Benjamin Franklin but to the conceptualization of the national literature.

Philadelphia, Pennsylvania
March, 1980

AUTHOR'S NOTE TO THE 1887 EDITION

——◆——

My thanks are due to Dr. Samuel Green, of the Massachusetts Historical Society; to Mr. Theodore Dwight, of the Library of the Department of State at Washington; to Mr. Hildeburn, of the Philadelphia Athenæum; and especially to Mr. Lindsay Swift, of the Boston Public Library, and Mr. F. D. Stone, of the Pennsylvania Historical Society, for the help so kindly given me when gathering the material for this Life of Franklin.

JOHN BACH McMASTER.

Philadelphia,
October, 1887.

BENJAMIN FRANKLIN

CHAPTER I.

1706–1723.

THE story of the life of Benjamin Franklin begins at a time when Queen Anne still ruled the colonies; when the colonies were but ten in number, and when the population of the ten did not sum up to four hundred thousand souls; at a time when witches were plentiful in New England; when foxes troubled the farmers of Lynn; when wolves and panthers abounded in Connecticut; when pirates infested the Atlantic coast; when there was no such thing as a stage-coach in the land; when there were but three colleges and one newspaper in the whole of British North America; when no printing-press existed south of Philadelphia; when New York was still defended by a high stockade; and when Ann Pollard, the first white woman that ever set foot on the soil of Boston, was still enjoying a hale old age.

On the January morning, 1706, when Franklin received his name in the Old South Church at Boston, the French had not founded the city of Mobile nor the city of New Orleans, nor begun the construction of that great chain of forts which stretched across our country from the St. Lawrence to the Gulf. Philip Jones had not marked out the streets of Baltimore; the proprietors of Carolina had not surrendered their charter, and the colony was still governed on the absurd plan of Locke; Delaware was still the property of William Penn; the founder of Georgia was a lad of eighteen. Of the few places that deserved to be called towns, the largest was Boston. Yet the area of Boston was less than one square mile, and the population did not equal ten thousand souls. The chief features of the place were three hills, since greatly cut down; three coves, long since filled up; the patch of common, where the cows fed at large; and the famous Neck. Across the Neck was a barrier, the gate of which was closed each night at nine, and never opened on the Sabbath. Behind the barrier was a maze of narrow streets, lined with buildings most of which have long since disappeared. On the site of the Old South Church stood a wooden meeting-house, pulled down in 1729. Near by were the pillory and the stocks, and just over the way on Milk Street was the humble dwelling of Josiah Franklin and Abiah Folger his wife.

Josiah was an Englishman, a dissenter, and a dyer; came to Boston in 1685, and, finding no use for his trade, abandoned it and became a tallow-chandler instead. Abiah Folger was his second wife. The first wife brought him seven children. Abiah brought him ten, and of her ten children Benjamin was the youngest son. This name was given him in honor of an uncle on the day of his birth, which, by the records of the Old South Church, must have been the sixth of January (Old Style), 1706.

Those were the days of compulsory education and compulsory thrift, the days when it was the duty of the selectmen to see that every Boston boy could read and write the English tongue, had some knowledge of the capital laws, knew by heart some orthodox catechism, and was brought up to do some honest work. Benjamin began his education at home; was sent when he was eight to the Latin School, and soon after to that of George Brownell, a pedagogue famed for his skill in arithmetic and the use of the quill. To this school he went regularly till the master ceased to teach

boys to make pot-hooks and loops, and began to
teach women to make new-fashioned purses and
to paint on glass, to do feather-work and fili-
gree and embroider a new way, to put Turkey
work on handkerchiefs, flowers on muslin, and
cover their short aprons with rich brocade ; till
he turned dressmaker and barber, made gowns
and furbelowed scarfs, and cut gentlewomen's
hair in the newest fashion.

When this change took place Benjamin was
ten. His schooling then ended, and for two
years he cut wicks, molded candles, tended shop,
ran on errands, and talked much of going to sea.
The parents had intended to breed him to the
church, and an uncle graciously promised to
leave him a bundle of sermons taken down from
time to time in short-hand.[1] But even this could
not move him. Benjamin remained steadfast;
and Josiah, alarmed at this fondness for ships
and sailors, determined to bind him to some
trade that should keep him on shore.

Like a man of sense, the father tried to find
the lad's bent, took him on long walks about
town, went among the bricklayers and the

[1] Three of the sermons taken down in this way are yet extant.
The title is, " *A Discourse on Forgiveness.* In Three Sermons
from Matt. vi. 15. By Nathaniel Vincent. Taken down in
short-hand by one of his hearers. Boston, J. Franklin, 1722."
The remarks " To the Reader " are signed B. F., and this
B. F. was undoubtedly Benjamin Franklin the elder.

joiners, the tanners and the cutlers, watched
him closely, and decided that he should become
a maker of knives. Benjamin was now sent to
a cousin who had learned the trade in London.
But a fee was asked. Josiah was vexed, and
the boy was soon home and in the shop.

There he fell to reading. As to the character of the books that made the library of Josiah
Franklin, neither his will, inventory, nor account
afford much information. From the inventory
it appears that he died possessed of two large
bibles, a concordance, " Willard's Body of Di-
vinity," and " a parcel of small books." But
we gather from the autobiography of Benjamin
that the collection of books that lay upon the
shelves was, with a few exceptions, such as no
boy of our time thinks of reading ; such as cannot be found even in the libraries of students
uncovered with dust; such as are rarely seen in
the catalogues of book auctions, and never come
into the hands of bookbinders to be reclothed.
There were, Mather's " Essay to do Good,"
and Defoe's " Essay on Projects," Plutarch's
" Lives," the only readable book in the collection, and a pile of thumbed and dog-eared pamphlets on polemical theology such as any true
son of the dissenting church might read ; such
as those in which Increase Mather and Solomon
Stoddart discussed the grave questions, Can bap-

tized persons destitute of religion come to the
table of the Lord? Is it lawful to wear long
hair? At what time of evening does the Sabbath
begin? Is it lawful for men to set their dwelling-
houses at such a distance from the place of public worship that they and their families cannot
well attend it? Uninviting as this literature
may seem, Franklin read it with pleasure, for
he was by nature a debater and a disputatious
man. Indeed, there is much reason to believe
that he was himself the author of an eight-page
tract ridiculing some of Stoddart's remarks, and
called " Hooped Petticoats Arraigned and Condemned by the Light of Nature and the Law
of God."

These books finished, he determined to get
more. Borrow he could not. He knew no
bookseller, and a circulating library did not
exist anywhere in America. In a room in the
Town Hall at Boston were gathered a few volumes which, in old wills, old letters, and the
diaries of prominent men, is called the " Public
Library." But there is not any reason to suppose that one of the books could have been
carried home by a tallow-chandler's son, or
treated of any subject less serious than religion.
In the whole town there was not, in all likelihood, a solitary copy of any of the works of one
of that glorious band of writers who made the

literature of the reign of Queen Anne so famous. The first catalogue of Harvard Library
was printed in 1723, yet there is not in it the
title of any of the works of Addison, of any of
the satires of Swift, of any of the poems of Pope,
of any of the writings of Bolingbroke or Dry-
den, Steele, Prior, or Young. The earliest copy
of Shakespeare brought to America was of the
edition of 1709. No copy was ever advertised
for sale till 1722. Even such books as Harvard
did own, it was seriously urged, should, after
the manner of the Bodleian Library, be chained
to the desk.

Nor did the boy fare much better when,
with the few halfpence he had saved, he went
among the booksellers to buy. The steam
printing-press has, in our time, placed within
reach of the poorest office-boy the most delightful works of poetry and travel, of history and
biography, of essay and fiction, the languages of
ten civilized nations can afford. When Franklin began to read, a printing-press was a "raree
show." Neither in New Hampshire, nor Rhode
Island, nor New Jersey, nor Delaware had such
a thing been seen. He was three years old before a type was set in Connecticut. He was
twenty when the first press reached Maryland.
He was twenty-three before one was perma-
nently set up in Virginia, and another year

passed by before a printer appeared in the Carolinas. In the four colonies where there were printers, the press was busy in the cause of the church. Between the first of January, 1706, and the first of January, 1718, all the publications known to have been printed in America number at least five hundred and fifty. Of these but eighty-four are not on religious topics, and of the eighty-four, forty-nine are almanacs. " The Origin of the Whalebone Petticoat;" ' The Simple Cobbler of Agawam in America;" John Williams's " Redeemed Captive Returning to Zion," an Indian story, which for a time was more sought after than Mather's " Treacle fetched out of a Viper;" Mary Rowlandson's " Captivity among the Indians," and " Entertaining Passages relating to Philip's War," were the only approaches made in all these years to what would now be called light literature.

Among the four hundred and sixty-six books of a religious tone, by far the best was " Pilgrim's Progress," printed at Boston in 1681 and reprinted in 1706. A copy of this was Benjamin's first purchase; was read, reread, and sold, and, with the money and a few more pence he had saved, forty volumes of Burton's "Historical Collections" were secured. The bent of his mind was now unmistakable. He stood in no danger of going to sea; he did not need his uncle's sermons; he would never be content to mold candles nor grind knives. For the lad who could deny himself the few treats afforded by a Puritan town, save his coppers and lay them out on such books as were then to be had at Boston, there seemed to be but one career, the career of a man of letters.

No such man had then appeared in the colonies. The greatest American then living was unquestionably Cotton Mather. Yet he is in no sense deserving to be called a man of letters. His pen, indeed, was never idle. Four hundred and twenty-three of his productions are still extant, yet our literature would have suffered no loss if every one of them had perished. Everything that he left is of value, but the value is of that kind which belongs to a bit of the Charter Oak; to a sword worn by Miles Standish; to an uncomfortable chair in which Governor Bradford sat; or to a broken plate used by the Pilgrims on their voyage to Plymouth. To hurry through a volume and write a sermon was, with Mather, a morning's work. To preach seventy sermons in public, forty more in private, publish fourteen pamphlets, keep thirty vigils and sixty fasts, and still have time for persecuting witches, was nothing unusual for him to do in a year. The habit of starving the body to purify the soul he adopted when a lad of fourteen, and in the fifty-two years that remained to him his fasts were more than four hundred and fifty. Sometimes they numbered ten a week. Often they lasted three days. On all such occasions he would lie face downward on his study-floor, fasting, weeping, praying, calling on the name of God. By the time he was forty, even such mortification was not enough for him, and he began to keep vigils; then he would leave his bed at the dead of night, fall prostrate on the floor of his library, and spend the hours of darkness " wrestling with God " and getting " unutterable communications from Heaven." The simplest act of life was to Mather an occasion for religious meditation. When he mended his fire he remembered that godliness should flame up within him. When he washed his hands he recalled that a pure heart was also required of the citizen of Zion. When he pared his nails he reflected on the duty of putting away all superfluity of naughtiness. If a tall man passed him on the street he would exclaim, " Lord, give that man high attainments in Christianity." When he saw a lame man he would say, " Lord, help him to walk uprightly." In early life Mather stuttered and stammered, and spoke with difficulty. Thinking himself unfit to serve the Lord, he began to fit himself to serve man, and studied medicine. But an old schoolmaster cured him of stuttering; he began to preach, and is now remembered for the support he gave to inoculation, to the witchcraft delusion of 1692, and to the censorship of the press James Franklin and his apprentice Benjamin did so much to destroy.

It was in 1718, when he had just turned twelve, that Benjamin was bound to his brother, who a year later began to print the second newspaper in America. Not many years ago the historian of the town of Salem, while rummaging among the records of the Colonial State Paper Office at London, brought to light a small four-page sheet entitled " Publick Occurrences, Both Foreign and Domestick." The date was Thursday, September 25, 1690; the size of each page was seven inches by eleven, and one of the four was blank. The purpose of " Publick Occurrences " was praiseworthy. He wished, the printer declared, to do " something towards the curing, or at least the charming, of the spirit of lying; " and he should, he promised, put forth an issue once each month, unless a " glut of occurrences " required it oftener. Four days later the General Court decided that " Publick Occurrences " was a pamphlet, that it contained reflections of a high nature, that it was printed contrary to law, and that henceforth nothing should come from the press till a license had first been obtained. None was ever issued for the offending pamphlet, and, save that at London, no copy of it has since been seen.

"Publick Occurrences" is commonly believed to have been the first newspaper in our country. It might more truly be called the first magazine, for it was, as the General Court declared, a pamphlet. The true newspaper did not appear for fourteen years, and was then begun by the Boston postmaster. The duties of his place were far from exacting. If he opened his office on Monday of each week from seven to twelve for the distribution of letters the riders brought in, and again from two to seven for the reception of letters the riders were to take out, collected postage once a quarter, made a list of letters not called for, and higgled with ship-captains for distributing letters they ought to have lodged with him, he did all he was required to do.

To John Campbell, however, these duties were not enough, and to them he added those of a gatherer of news. He visited every stranger that came to town, boarded every ship that entered the bay, collected what scraps of news he could, and wrote them out in a fair hand for the public good. Copies of his " News Letter " passed from hand to hand at the Coffee House, found their way to the neighboring towns, and went out in the mail to the governors of the New England colonies. As time passed, the glut of occurrences steadily increased; his work grew daily more in favor; and he was at last compelled to lay down the pen, betake himself to type, and become the founder of the American newspaper. Monday, the seventeenth of April, 1704, was a white day in the annals of Boston, and as the printer struck off the first copy of the first number of the "Boston News Letter," Chief Justice Sewell, who stood by, seized the paper and bore it, damp from the press, to the President of Harvard College. Some extracts from the "Flying Post" concerning the Pretender, the text of a sermon licensed to be printed, notices of a couple of arrivals, of a couple of deaths, of the appointment of an admiralty judge and deputy, and a call for business, is all it contains.

During fifteen years the "News Letter" had no rival. But in 1719 Campbell lost the post-office, refused in revenge to have his newspapers carried by the riders, and the new postmaster at once established the "Boston Gazette," and gave the matter to James Franklin to print. While engaged in setting type and mixing ink in his brother's office, Benjamin

began to write. His first attempts were two
ballads in doggerel verse, treating of subjects
which at that time filled the popular mind. The
keeper of the Boston light had been drowned
in a storm. A pirate renowned along the whole
coast had been killed.

There is not now living a man who has ever
beheld such a rover out of the China seas.
Early in the eighteenth century the black flag
had been seen by scores of captains who went
in and out of the colonial ports. From the
West Indies, from New Providence, from the
sounds and inlets of the Virginia coast, from
Cape Fear River, from Pamlico Sound, from
the very shores of Massachusetts, freebooter
after freebooter sallied forth to plunder and
destroy. When Captain Kidd died in 1700,
Quelch succeeded him, and long found shelter
in the bays and harbors of New England. In
one of them, on a return from a prosperous
coasting trip, the people surprised him, and
hanged him with six companions on the banks
of Charles River, June 30, 1704. The event is
memorable as it became the occasion of the
first piece of newspaper reporting in America.
In the crowd that stood about the gallows-tree
that day in June was John Campbell, who, in
the next number of the " News Letter," described the scene, " the exhortation to the mal-

efactors," and the prayer put up for the culprits' repose, " as nearly," says he, " as it could be taken down in writing in a great crowd."

From the moment such a character fell into the clutches of the law he became the victim of the most terrible religious enginery the colony could produce. His trial was speedy. His conviction was sure. His sentence was imposed by the judge in a long sermon after a long prayer, and he was, on the Sunday or the Thursday before execution, brought to the meeting-house loaded with chains, and placed in the front seats, to be reprobated and held up by name to the whole congregation behind him. The day of his death was a gala day. The entire town marched in procession behind his coffin to the foot of the Common, to Boston Neck, or to Broughton's Hill on the Charles River, where stood the gallows, from one end of which floated a huge black flag adorned with a figure of Death holding a dart in one hand and an hour-glass in the other. There, after just such prayers and exhortations as Campbell has described, the pirate would be left swinging in his chains.

Next in turn came Bellamy, the terror of every New England sailor till in 1717 he was wrecked on Cape Cod, where such of his crew as did not perish in the sea were hanged.

When George I. came to the throne New Providence was a nest of pirates, and thither a ship of war was sent to drive them out. Two sought refuge in Cape Fear River, a third took up his abode among the people of Pamlico Sound. There, protected by the governor, dreaded by the people, he squandered in riot and debauchery his ill-gotten wealth. When all was gone, Theach went back to his roving life, gathered a crew, procured a ship, cleared her as a merchantman, and was again a pirate chief. In a few weeks he was home with a rich cargo in a fine French ship. He swore the vessel had been picked up at sea. But the people knew better, sent Governor Spottiswoode word, and a man-of-war soon appeared in Pamlico Sound. Theach descried her one evening in November, 1718, and the next morning a running fight took place through the sounds and inlets of that singular coast. Discipline prevailed; the pirate was boarded, and as Theach, covered with wounds and surrounded by the dead, stepped back match in hand to fire a pistol, he fainted and fell upon the deck.

The Christian name of Theach was John; but among the wretches who manned his guns and furled his sails, and the captains who fled in terror from his flag, he passed by the name of Blackbeard. He was a boy's ideal of a pirate chief. His brow was low; his eyes were small; his huge, shaggy beard, black as a coal, hung far down upon his breast. Over his shoulders were three braces of pistols; in battle, lighted matches stuck out from under his hat and protruded from behind his ears. In his fits of rage he became a demon. But his hours of good-nature were more to be feared than his moments of fury. Sometimes he would amuse the boon-companions of his crew by shooting out the light of his cabin; sometimes he would send balls whizzing past the ears or through the hair of those who sat with him at table. To mimic the Devil was a favorite sport, and on one occasion, to give greater reality to his impersonation, the hatches were battened down and the crew half stifled with the fumes of sulphur.

The death of such a character in a hand-to-hand conflict on the deck of his own ship was as fine a subject for song as a writer of ballads could desire. The street ballad was then and long remained the chief source of popular information. If a great victory were won on land or sea; if a murder were committed; if a noted criminal were hanged; if a highwayman were caught; if a ship were wrecked; if a good man died; if a sailor came back from the Spanish main with some strange tale of adventure, a ballad-monger was sure to put the details into doggerel rhyme, and the event became fixed in the mind of the people. The influence of such verses was great and lasting, the demand for them was incessant, and the printer who could furnish a steady supply was sure of a rich return. Thomas Fleet is said to have made no small part of his fortune by the sale of ballads his press struck off. James Franklin, with a like purpose in view, bade his apprentice turn his knack of rhyming to some use, suggested the themes, and when the ballads were printed sent Benjamin forth to hawk them in the street. That upon the drowning of the light-keeper and his family sold prodigiously, for the event was recent and the man well known; yet not a line of it remains.

From the manufacture of ballad poetry Benjamin was saved by his father, who told him plainly that all poets were beggars, and that he would do well to turn his time and talents to better use. The advice was taken, and Benjamin went on with his reading. An intense longing for books possessed him. When he had secured one, he read and reread it till he obtained another, and to get others he shrewdly gained the friendship of some booksellers' apprentices and persuaded them, in his behalf, to commit temporary theft. Urged on by him, night after night they purloined from their masters' shelves such books as he wanted, and left them with him to read. Some were perused at leisure; some that could not long be spared were taken after the shutters were up in the evening and returned in the morning before the shutters were down. Then he would sit up till the dawn was soon to break, reading by the light of a farthing candle made in his father's shop.

Everything that he read at this time of life influenced him strongly. A wretched book on vegetable diet came into his hands, and he at once began to live on rice, potatoes, and hasty-pudding. He read Xenophon's " Memorabilia," and ever after used the Socratic method of dispute; he read Shaftesbury and Collins, and became a skeptic; he read a volume of Addison, and gained a delightful style.

As first published, the " Spectator " appeared in seven volumes, and of these, after many vicissitudes, the third crossed the Atlantic and fell in the way of Franklin. No one knew the contents of the Boston bookshops better than he. Yet the volume was, he tells us, the first of the series he had seen. It is not unlikely that another copy could not then be found in the province of Massachusetts Bay. However this may be, Franklin had now read the book which affected him far more deeply than anything else he read to his dying day. Lad though he was, the rare wit, the rich humor, the grace of style, the worldly wisdom of the "Spectator," amazed and delighted him. After nightfall, on Sundays, in the early morning, whenever he had a moment to spare, the book was before him. Again and again he read the essays and determined to make them his model. He would take some number that particularly pleased him, jot down the substance of each sentence, put by the notes, and, after a day or two, reproduce the essay in language of his own. This practice convinced him that his great want was a stock of words, and he at once began to turn the tales into verse. The search after words that would not change the sense, yet were of length to suit the meter and of sound to suit the rhyme, was, he felt sure, the best way to supply the deficiency.

When his vocabulary had been enlarged, Franklin began to study arrangement of thought. Then he would put down his notes in any order, and after a while seek to rearrange the sentences in the order of the essay. Next he fell to reading books on navigation and arithmetic, rhetoric and grammar, Locke "On the Human Understanding," and "The Art of Thinking," by the members of Port Royal. Some of these he bought. The money to buy with was obtained by persuading the brother to give him half the shillings paid out in board and let him board himself, by putting in practice a theory of vegetable diet, by refusing meat and fish, eating bread and biscuit, and so saving a little even of the pittance.

Thus equipped, Benjamin began his literary career at the age of fifteen. After holding office seven months, the successor of John Campbell was turned out, the "Boston Gazette" passed to other hands, James Franklin ceased to print it, and amazed the town by starting a newspaper of his own. The name of this weekly was the "New England Courant." In point of time it came fourth in the colonies, for, the day before the first number was seen at Boston, Bradford's "American Mercury" appeared at Philadelphia. In quality the "Courant" was the most readable, the most entertaining, the most aggressive newspaper of the four. Precisely what the early numbers contained cannot now be known, for not an impression of a number earlier than the eighteenth is extant. It is certain, however, that they were filled with sprightly contributions from a set of young men who, weary of the dullness of the "News Letter" and the "Gazette," came to the office of James Franklin and supplied the "Courant" with what passed for wit. They were, we are told, young doc-

tors, and had picked up some knowledge of
medicine by watching the barbers cup and let
blood, and by pounding drugs and serving as
apprentices in the offices of physicians of the
town.

Though their knowledge of physic was small,
their impudence was great, and the "Courant," before the fourth number was reached,
had plunged into a warm dispute over the
greatest medical discovery of the age. What
Lady Mary Wortley Montagu had done for
Europe, Cotton Mather was doing for America.
He had read in the "Transactions of the Royal
Society" of the wonders of inoculation, believed
in it, and was urging and begging his townsmen
to submit to a trial. Indeed, he was demon-
strating the efficacy of the preventive before
their very eyes. But for his pains they rewarded
him as every man has been rewarded who ever
yet bestowed any blessing on the human race.
He was called a fool. He was pronounced mad.
He was told that the smallpox, which that
very year was carrying off one in every thir-
teen of the inhabitants of Boston, was a scourge
sent from God, and that to seek to check it was
impious. One wretch flung a lighted hand-
grenade, with some vile language attached,
through a window of Mather's house. The
"Courant" declared that inoculation was from

the devil. Were not the ministers for it, and
did not the devil often use good men to spread
his delusions on the world? Increase Mather
called this " a horrid thing to be related ;" said,
with truth, that he had seen the time when the
civil government would have speedily put down
such "a cursed libel;" withdrew his subscription, and sent his grandson each week to the
office to buy a copy of the sheet. Cotton Mather
applied to the "Courant" such epithets as he
might have used in speaking of a book by Calef.
The newspaper was, he said, "full freighted
with nonsense, unmanliness, raillery, profane-
ness, immorality, arrogance, calumnies, lies, con-
tradictions, and whatnot." The whole town
was divided. Some remonstrated with James
Franklin on the street. Some attacked him in
the "News Letter" and the "Gazette." So
many hastened to support him that forty new
subscribers were secured in a month. Such an
increase was great, for no newspaper then
pretended to have a circulation of three hundred copies.

It was at this time, while the dispute with the
Mathers was warmest, that some manuscript
was found one morning on the printing-house
floor. Benjamin wrote it, and modestly thrust
it under the door during the night. The "Autobiography" makes no mention of what these

sheets contained, but there is much reason to believe that the manuscript was the first of those brief letters with which for six months Silence Dogood amused the readers of the "Courant."

The Dogood papers find no place in any of Franklin's collected writings. They were not even ascribed to him till Mr. Parton wrote his biography. But, in the notes and memoranda jotted down by Franklin when about to write the "Autobiography," he claims the Dogood papers as his own. They are clearly Franklin's work; and so well did the lad catch the spirit, the peculiar diction, the humor of his model, the "Spectator," that he seems to have written with a copy of Addison open before him. "I have observed," says the short-faced gentleman in the opening paragraph of the first number of the "Spectator," "that a reader seldom peruses a book with pleasure till he knows whether the writer of it be a black or a fair man, of a mild or a choleric disposition, married or a bachelor, with other peculiarities of a like nature that conduce very much to a right understanding of an author." "As the generality of people," says Mrs. Dogood in the opening paragraph of the first of her epistles, "now-a-days are unwilling either to commend or dispraise what they read till they are in some manner informed who or what the author of it is, whether he be rich or poor, old or young, a scholar or a leather-apron man, it will not come amiss to give some account of my past life." She thereupon proceeds to inform her readers that she was in youth an orphan bound out apprentice to a country parson ; that he had carefully educated her, and, after many vain attempts to get a wife from among the topping sort of people, had married her. She was now his widow, but might be persuaded to change her state if she could only be sure of getting a good-humored, sober, agreeable man. Till then, she should content herself with the company of her neighbor Rusticus and the town minister Clericus, who lodged with her, and who would from time to time beautify her writings with passages from the learned tongues. Such selections would be both ornamental and fashionable, and to those igno-rant of the classics, pleasing in the extreme. To please and amuse was her purpose. Her themes therefore would be as various as her letters, for whoever would please all must be now merry and diverting, now solemn and serious ; one while sharp and biting, then sober and religious ; ready to write now on poli-tics and now on love. Thus would each reader find something agreeable to his fancy, and in his turn be pleased.

True to this plan, essays, dreams, criticisms, humorous letters came forth at least once a fortnight, till the Dogood papers numbered fourteen. A talk with Clericus on academic education produces a dream, in which Franklin gives vent to the hatred he felt towards Harvard College. A wretched elegy on the death of Mehitabel Kitel suggests a receipt for a New England funeral elegy, and some ridicule on that kind of poetry he calls Kitelic. Now his theme is "Pride and Hoop Petticoats," now "Nightwalkers," now "Drunkenness," now a plan for the relief of those unhappy women who, as a punishment for the pride and insolence of youth, are forced to remain old maids. One week Silence sent an abstract from the "London Journal." The subject was "Freedom of Thought," and, whether written by Benjamin or really borrowed from the "Journal," the article had a special meaning; for James Franklin was at that very time undergoing punishment for exercising freedom of thought.

On the twenty-second of May, 1722, a piratical brigantine with fifty men and four swivel guns appeared off Block Island, took several ships and crews, and began depredations which extended along the New England coast. News of the pirate was quickly sent to Governor Shute of Massachusetts, and by him transmitted to the Council on the seventh of June. The next day the House of Representatives resolved to dispatch Captain Peter Papillon in a vessel, strongly armed and manned, in pursuit of the rover; offered a bounty of ten pounds for each pirate killed; and decreed that the ship and cargo of the rovers should be the property of the captors.

The number of the "Courant" containing the sixth of the Dogood papers announced under "Boston News" that the vessel fitted out by the government would sail on the eleventh of June. But elsewhere, in a pretended letter from Newport, were these words : "The government of the Massachusetts are fitting out a ship to go after the Pirates, to be commanded by Captain Peter Papillon, and 'tis thought he will sail some time this month if wind and weather permit."

For this piece of harmless fun the Council summoned James Franklin before them, questioned him sharply, and voted the paragraph "a high affront to this Government." The House of Representatives concurred, and bade the sheriff, under the speaker's warrant, seize James Franklin and lodge him in the stone jail. There for a month he languished, while Benjamin conducted the business of the printing-house and published the "Courant."

With each succeeding issue the newspaper
grew more tantalizing, more exasperating, till
in January, 1723, James Franklin a second
time felt the strong hand of the law. The
real cause of displeasure was some remarks on
the behavior of Governor Shute, one of the
many arrant fools a series of stupid English
kings sent over to govern the colonies. He
quarreled with the General Court because it
would not suffer him to approve or disapprove
the speaker; because it ventured to appoint
public fasts; interrupted its sessions by long
adjournments; suspended military officers, and
assumed the direction of Indian wars; and
when he could contain himself no longer, he
suddenly set off for England. Of this the
" Courant " had something to say.

Could any one, it was asked, suppose that
the departure of the governor for England
with so much privacy and displeasure was
likely to promote the welfare of the province
when he reached the British court? Would
it not be well to send one or two persons of
known ability, and born in the province, to the
British court, there to vindicate the conduct
of the House of Representatives since the late
misunderstanding? Ought the ministers to
pray for Samuel Shute, Esquire, as immediate
governor, and at the same time for the lieu-

tenant-governor as commander-in-chief? Was
not praying for the success of his voyage, if, as
many supposed, he wished to hurt the province,
praying in effect for the destruction of the province? The pretended cause of offense was an
essay on religious hypocrisy. For publishing
this, James Franklin was forbidden by the General Court to "print or publish the New England Courant, or any other such pamphlet or
paper of a like nature, except it be first supervised by the Secretary of the Province."

In this strait the printer called his friends
about him for advice. Were the order to be
obeyed; were James Franklin to go once each
week to the office of the secretary, show his
manuscript, and ask leave to publish a column
or two of extracts from London newspapers
five months old, some fulsome praise of Governor Shute, two or three advertisements for
the apprehension of runaway apprentices and
as many more for runaway slaves, the "Courant" would, they felt, fall at once to the level
of the "News Letter" and the "Gazette," and
die of dullness in a month. Change the publisher and this would be avoided, and the "Courant" could continue to be as impudent as ever,
for the order applied to James Franklin and to
him alone. His friends therefore urged him to
make the change; their advice was taken, and

the "Courant" of February 4th–11th, 1723, contains this falsehood: "The late Printer of this paper, finding so many Inconveniences would arise by his carrying the Manuscript and Public news to be supervised by the Secretary as to render his carrying it on unprofitable, has entirely dropt the undertaking." Thenceforth the newspaper issued under Benjamin Franklin's name. The public were assured the late printer had abandoned the enterprise entirely. Lest anyone should inquire into the truth of this statement, the old indenture was cancelled and Benjamin declared free. But the elder brother had no intention of freeing his apprentice, and the cancelled indenture was replaced by a new one which the brothers kept carefully concealed.

It was now pretended that the "Courant" was conducted by a "Club for the Propagation of Sense and Good Manners among the docible part of Mankind in His Majestys Plantations in America." Of this club Dr. Janus was perpetual dictator, and of Dr. Janus an account was given in a humorous "Preface" which Benjamin wrote for the first number of the "Courant" printed in his own name.

"The Society," he wrote, had "design'd to present the Public with the effigies of Dr. Janus; but the Limner, to whom he was presented for a draught of his Countenance discried (and this he is ready to offer upon Oath) nineteen features in his face more than ever he beheld in any Human Visage before; which so raised the price of his Picture that our Master himself forbid the extravagance of coming up to it. And then besides, the Limner objected to a Schism in his Face which splits it from his Forehead in a Straight line down to his chin in such wise that Mr. Painter protests 'tis a double face and will have four pounds for its portraiture. However tho' this double face has spoilt us a pretty Picture, yet we all rejoice to see old Janus in our company. . . . As for his morals he is a chearly Christian as the Country Phrase has it. A man of good temper, courteous Deportment, sound Judgement; a mortal Hater of Nonsense, Foppery, Formality and endless ceremony." To him all letters must be addressed, and thenceforth not a number of the " Courant " issues without some pretended communication " To the Venerable Old Janus," " To Good Master Janus," " To the ancient and venerable Dr. Janus," " To Old Janus the Couranteer." " The gentle reader," " the ingenuous and courteous reader," is assured that the " design of the Club is to contribute to the diversion and Merryment of the town," that " pieces of pleasantry and Mirth have a secret charm in them to allay the heats and Tumors of our Spirits and make us forget our restless resentments, and that no paper shall be suffered to pass without a latin motto if one can possibly be found. Such mottoes charm the Vulgar and give the learned the pleasure of construing. Gladly would the Club add a scrap or two of Greek; but the printer, unhappily has no type. The candid reader therefore will not impute this defect to ignorance; for Docter Janus knows all the Greek letters by heart."

Under the management of the club, the "Courant" grew daily in favor. Each week the list of subscribers became longer, the borrowers became more numerous, and the advertisements steadily increased. Flushed with success, Benjamin in a humorous notice informed his readers that the club had raised the price of the paper to twelve shillings a year. And well he might, for so sprightly and entertaining a newspaper did not exist anywhere else in the colonies. But for this prosperity James Franklin was soon to pay dearly. The very act by which he evaded the order of the General Court placed him in the power of his apprentice, and set the lad an example of dishonesty which Benjamin was quick to follow. From the few glimpses we obtain of James Franklin in the " Autobiography " of Benjamin, he seems

to have been a man morose, ill-tempered,
doomed not to succeed. The "Junto" knew,
and he must have known, that no journeyman
in his printing-house did such work, and that
no contributor to the paper wrote such pieces
as his young brother. Had he been a man of
sense and judgment, he would undoubtedly have
cancelled the indentures in all honesty, given
the lad his freedom, and made him a partner.
But he took precisely the opposite course.
The more the apprentice displayed his ability,
the more domineering became the master.
From disputes the two proceeded to quarrels,
and from quarrels to blows. Then Benjamin
turned to the cancelled indentures and declared
himself free. Unable to deny this, James went
among the printers and persuaded them to refuse his brother work, and advertised in the
"Courant" for "a likely lad for an apprentice." Benjamin, after selling a few of his
books for ready money, turned his back upon
Boston and ran away.

A packet sloop carried him to New York.
There he sought out William Bradford, still
remembered as the man who put up the first
press, set the first type, and printed the first
pamphlet, in the middle colonies. Bradford
could give the boy no work, and recommended
him to go on to Philadelphia. He set out ac-

cordingly, was almost lost in a storm in New York Bay, landed at Perth Amboy, and went across New Jersey on foot.

There were at that day but two roads across New Jersey between Philadelphia and New York. One, long known as the Old Road, ran out from Elizabethtown Point to what is now New Brunswick, thence in an almost direct line to the Delaware above Trenton, and so on to Burlington, where the traveler once a week took boat to Philadelphia. But it was long after Franklin's boyhood before the road became anything better than a bridle-path, or before a wagon of any kind rolled over it. So late as 1716, when the Assembly fixed the ferry rate at New Brunswick, two tolls only were established, one " for horse and man," and one for " single persons." Ten pounds, raised each year by tax on the innkeepers of Piscataway, Woodbridge, and Elizabethtown, were thought ample to keep the pathway in repair.

The favored road across the province was that from Perth Town to Burlington, on the Delaware, and was, as early as 1707, wide enough for a wagon to pass without scraping the hubs on the trees. In that year the Assembly complained as a great evil that a patent had been given to several persons to carry goods by wagon over the Amboy road to the exclusion of the Old Road. But the governor reminded the grumblers that by this means a trade had grown up between Philadelphia, Burlington, Perth Town, and New York such as had never before existed.

Notwithstanding this travel, the road when Franklin used it ran for miles through an uninhabited country. The almanacs, which were the road-books of that day, make mention of but four places where a traveler could find rest and refreshment. One was at Cranberry Brook; another was at Allentown, a place nine years old. A third was at Crosswick Bridge; and the fourth at Dr. Brown's, eight miles from Burlington, and here Benjamin slept on the night of his second day from Amboy.

Early the next morning he was at Burlington, where he once more took boat, slept that night in the fields, and early one Sunday morning in October, 1723, entered Philadelphia. For a while he wandered about the streets, but falling in with a number of Quakers, followed them to meeting and there fell asleep. It was well that he did, for had the constable met him sauntering around the town, Benjamin would have been placed in the lockup.

CHAPTER II.

THE prospect that lay before Benjamin, when, the fatigue of the journey slept off, he went forth in search of work, was poor indeed. All the printing done in Pennsylvania was done on the press of Andrew Bradford; and all the printing Bradford did in a year could, in our time, be done in one hour. From his press came the "American Weekly Mercury," the contents of which would not fill a column and a half of such a daily newspaper as the "Boston Traveller" or the "Philadelphia Press." Never in any one year did all the tracts, all the sermons, all the almanacs, all the appeals, catechisms, and proposals published in Pennsylvania number thirty-nine. Nor did the largest book yet printed contain three hundred small octavo pages. Indeed, forty-seven years had not gone since William Bradford began the list of Middle Colony publications with Atkins's "Kalendarium Pennsilvaniense, being an Almanac for the year of Grace 1686."

William Bradford was then a lad of two-and-twenty, who had been brought up to set type and work a press in the shop of Andrew Sowle, a famous London printer of Friends' books. His relations with Sowle, first as apprentice and then as son-in-law, brought him often to the notice of William Penn. Anxious to secure a good printer for his province, Penn made an offer to Bradford to go to Pennsylvania and print the laws: the offer was accepted, and in the summer of 1685 the young printer landed at Philadelphia with types, a press, and three letters from George Fox.

On the day he landed there were but two printing-presses in the whole of British North America. Evidence exists that there was, for a while, a third; that in 1682 one John Buckner published the Virginia laws of 1680; that he was promptly summoned before the governor and council, censured, and forbidden to print again till the king's will was known; and that for forty-seven years not another type was set in the Old Dominion. With the single exception of the Virginia laws of 1680, not a piece of printing had been done out of Cambridge, Massachusetts, when early in December, 1685, Bradford issued the " Kalendarium Pennsilvaniense," and introduced "the great art and mystery of printing " into the Middle Colonies.

" Some Irregularities," said he in his address to
the readers, " there be in this Diary, which I
desire you to pass by this year ; for being lately
come hither, my Materials were Misplaced and
out of order." But the advance sheet had
no sooner been seen by Secretary Markham
than he detected one irregularity for which
neither the recent arrival nor the disordered
fonts could atone. " In the Chronology,"
Markham informed the council, " of the Al-
manack sett forth by Samuel Atkins of Philadelphia and by William Bradford of the same
place, are the words 'the beginning of Government by ye Lord Penn.'" Thereupon the
council sent for Atkins and bade him "blott
out ye words Lord Penn;" and to "Will
Bradford, ye printer, gave Charge not to print
anything but what shall have lycense from ye
Council." Atkins obeyed, and in the only
copies of " Kalendarium " now extant the hated
words are blotted out.

With this the struggle for the liberty of the
press began in Pennsylvania. Twice was
Bradford called before the governor ; thrice
was he censured by the meeting ; once was he
put under heavy bonds, and once thrown into
jail, before he gathered his type, and in 1693
fastened his notice of removal on the court-
house door and set out for New York. Dur-

ing the six years that followed his departure not a type was set in Pennsylvania. Then the Friends brought out a press from London, put it under the censorship of a committee, and rented it to Reynier Jansen. Jansen died in 1705, and the press passed in turn to Tiberius Johnson, to Joseph Reyners, to Jacob Taylor, in whose hands it was when, in 1712, William Bradford established his son Andrew as a printer at Philadelphia.

For ten years Andrew Bradford continued to print almanacs and laws, religious tracts and political pamphlets, without a rival. But on the October morning, 1723, when Franklin passed under the sign of the Bible, entered the shop of Bradford and asked for work, Samuel Keimer, a rival printer, had set up in the town. Bradford had nothing for the lad to do, but gave him a home and sent him to Keimer, by whom he was soon employed. During a few months all went well, and Franklin spent his time courting, printing, and making friends. Among these was William Keith, who governed Pennsylvania for the children of Penn.

Keith affected great interest in the boy, and sent him to Boston with a letter urging Josiah to fit out the son as a master printer. Josiah refused, and Benjamin came back to Keith, who now dispatched him on a fool's errand to Lon-

don. He sailed with the belief that he was to
have letters of introduction and letters of
credit, that he was to buy types, paper, and a
press, and return to America a master printer.
He reached London to find Keith a knave and
himself a dupe.

Homeless, friendless, and with but fifteen
pistoles in his pocket, he now walked the
streets of London in search of work. This he
found at a great printing-house in Bartholomew
Close, and for a year toiled as compositor,
earning good wages and squandering them on
idle companions, lewd women, treats and
shows.

As he stood at the case it fell to his lot to
set type for Wollaston's "Religion of Nature
Delineated." No better specimen exists of the
theological writings of that day. It was the
forerunner of Butler's "Analogy" and Paley's
"Natural Theology." It was an attempt to
prove that, had the Bible never been written,
there would still be found in the natural world
around us manifest reasons for being regular at
church, for believing the soul to be immortal,
for not doing any of the innumerable things
the ten commandments forbid. As he composed the book, Franklin despised it, and soon
began to write a little pamphlet of his own in
refutation. The pamphlet he called "A Dis-

sertation on Liberty and Necessity, Pleasure and Pain." But when he had printed a hundred copies and given a few away, he grew ashamed of his own work, and so thoroughly suppressed it that but two copies of the original edition are now known to be extant. Were none in existence the loss would be trivial, for the pamphlet adds nothing to his just fame.

The pamphlet he divided in the true theological manner into two sections. One he called "Liberty and Necessity," and the other "Pleasure and Pain." "There is," said he, "a first Mover called God, the maker of all things. God is said to be all-wise, all-powerful, all-good. If he is all-wise, then whatever he does must be wise. If he is all-good, then whatever he does must be good. If he is all-powerful, then nothing can exist against his will; and as nothing can exist against his will, and, being all-good, he can will nothing but good, it follows that nothing but good can exist. Therefore evil does not exist. Again, if a creature is made by God, it must depend on God, and get its powers from him, and act always according to his will, because he is all-powerful. But, being all-good, his will is always for good, and the creature, being forced to obey it, can do nothing but what is good; and therefore evil does not exist. The creature, once more, being thus limited in its actions, being able to do only such things as God wills, can have no free will, liberty, or power to refrain from an action. But if there is no such thing as free will in creatures, there can be neither merit nor demerit in their actions; therefore every creature must be equally esteemed by God."

This much settled, Franklin proceeds to the second part, on Pleasure and Pain. " Every creature," says he, "is capable of feeling uneasiness or pain. This pain produces desire to be freed from it in exact proportion to itself. The accomplishment of the desire produces an equal amount of pleasure. Pleasure therefore is equal to Pain. From all this it follows that Pleasure and Pain are inseparable and equal; that, being inseparable, no state of life can be happier than the present; that, being equal and contrary, they destroy each other, and that life therefore cannot be better than insensibility, for a creature that has ten degrees of pleasure taken from ten degrees of pain has nothing left, and is on an equality with a creature insensible to both."

The gist of his pamphlet may be briefly stated to be this : There are no future rewards and punishments, because all things and creatures are equally good and equally esteemed by God. There is no reason to believe that a future life can be happier than the present. There is no reason to believe in a future life. There is no reason to believe that man is any better than the brutes. There is no religion. Dr. Wollaston had declared, "The foundation of religion lies in that difference between the acts of men which distinguishes them into good, evil, indifferent." To prove that no such difference existed was the purpose of Franklin's essay.

Though the essay proved nothing, it brought him friends. Limited as the circulation was, a copy fell into the hands of the once famous author of "The Infallibility of Human Judgment." He admired the pamphlet, sought out Franklin and brought him to a club of skeptics that gathered nightly at "The Horns." There he met Bernard de Mandeville, who wrote "The Fable of the Bees," and Henry Pemberton, who still has a place in biographical dictionaries. Pemberton promised to introduce the lad to Isaac Newton, but the opportunity never served.

Irreligious, lewd, saving to very meanness, yet a spendthrift and a waste-all, the boy had now reached a crisis in his career. Ashamed of himself and of his life, a feeling of unrest took possession of him. In hopes of making better wages, he quit the printing-house in Bartholomew Close, and found employment at another near Lincoln's Inn Fields. Yet even this did not satisfy, and for one while he thought of setting up a swimming-school, and for another, of wandering over Europe supporting himself by his trade. From both of these follies he was saved by one Denman. Denman had once been a Bristol merchant; had failed, and emigrated to America; had retrieved his fortunes, and, to pay his debts, had gone back to England on the same ship with Franklin. It is certain that on one occasion Benjamin went to Denman for advice, and it is not unlikely that he now went again. However this may be, Denman gave him a clerkship, took him back to Philadelphia, and placed him in a shop. There, at twenty, the lad began to keep books, sell goods, learn the secrets of mercantile affairs, and was fast becoming a merchant, when his employer died, and he was forced to earn his bread as foreman of Keimer's establishment.

His duty at Keimer's was to reduce chaos to order, to mix ink, cast type, mend the presses, make cuts for the New Jersey paper-money bills, bind books, and watch the movements of the two redemptioners and three apprentices who served as compositors, pressmen, and devils. It was at this time that Benjamin founded the Junto, wrote his famous epitaph, grew religious, composed a liturgy for his own use, and became the father of an illegitimate son. The name of the mother most happily is not known; but as the law of bastardy was then rigidly enforced against the woman and not against the man, she was, in all likelihood, one of that throng who received their lashes in the market-place and filled the records of council with prayers for the remission of fines.

With Keimer, Franklin stayed but a little while. The two quarreled, parted, made up, and again separated, this time amicably, Keimer to go to destruction, Franklin to found a new printing-house and begin his great career. One of the three apprentices who stitched pamphlets and inked type was Hugh Meredith. This lad was country-bred, idle, cursed with an incurable longing for drink, and blessed with a father who for that day was more than well-to-do. Over the son, Franklin had great influence, had persuaded him to keep sober and be industrious, and the reward for these good deeds was now at hand. In one of the darkest hours of his life, when he had left Keimer in a passion, when Bradford could give him no work, when he thought seriously of wandering back to his father's house, Meredith visited him and proposed a partnership. The proposition was gladly accepted, the father of Meredith found the money, an order was sent to London for types and a press, and in the spring of 1728 the firm of Franklin & Meredith began business at "The New Printing-Office in High Street, near the Market."

Their first job was a hand-bill for a countryman. Their next was forty sheets of "The History of the Rise, Increase, and Progress of the Christian People called Quakers; Intermixed with Several Remarkable Occurrences. Written originally in Low Dutch and also translated into English, by William Sewel." A few copies having found their way to America, the Philadelphia meeting asked Bradford to reprint the book. Bradford cunningly asked time to consider, arranged with his aunt Tacy Sowle, the English publisher, for seven hundred copies, and then declined the proposition. The Friends thereupon turned to Keimer, who began the printing in 1725. But so great was the undertaking, and so ill was he equipped, that 1728 came and the history was not published. Nor would it have been in that year had not the last forty sheets and the index been sent to Franklin. We are told in the "Autobiography" that Breintnal procured them from the Quakers, but this is a mistake. They were sent by Keimer at the very time Franklin was roundly abusing him in the " Weekly Mercury."

Franklin next turned his attention to Bradford, to whom he had once been indebted for food and a home. Bradford was printer to the province, and in the gains of this post the new firm determined to share. When, therefore, the address of the governor issued, Franklin obtained a copy, printed it in much better form, laid a copy on the seat of each member of the Assembly, and thenceforth the public printing was his. Bradford was also printer of the " Weekly Mercury."

The " Mercury " was the only newspaper then published out of New England; was dull, but circulated from New York to Virginia, and paid well. As the new printing-office had little to do, Franklin determined to start a newspaper of his own, make it instructive and amusing, and share some of the profit Bradford alone enjoyed.

In an evil moment, however, he told his plan to George Webb, a foolish youth who had lately been an indentured servant of Keimer. The wretch hurried with the news to his former master, who took the hint, forestalled Franklin, and on December 28, 1728, issued number one of " The Universal Instructor in all Arts and Sciences and Pennsylvania Gazette." To have made a duller journal than Bradford's would have been impossible. It is small praise, there-fore, to say that Keimer's " Universal In-

structor " was by far the better of the two. No
one who reads the " Mercury " will ever accuse
Bradford of attempting anything but money-
making with the least possible exertion. Keimer
undoubtedly was just as eager to make money;
but, to do him justice, he strove at the same
time to amuse and instruct, and, clumsy as his
efforts were, they were laudable. To afford
instruction, he began the republication of Chambers's " Universal Dictionary of all the Arts and
Sciences," and started boldly with the letter A.
To afford amusement, a like use was made of
" The Religious Courtship " of De Foe, and of
some sketches of English life furnished by
Webb. Did Keimer expect to finish this task,
he must have looked forward to a long life for
the newspaper and himself. If so, he was
doomed to disappointment, for, when the fortieth number issued, the " Universal Instructor "
had passed into Franklin's hands.

The means taken to get the newspaper are
characteristic of his patience and his cunning.
Enraged at the duplicity of Keimer, he determined that the town should give this new venture no support. Having passed his apprentice-
ship in the midst of one newspaper controversy,
he knew that nothing lasting is ever gained
by calling hard names and indulging in vile
abuse; that if men came to the tavern to read

the "Instructor," or cancelled their subscriptions at the sign of the Bible, it was because they liked the "Instructor" better than the "Mercury;" and that the way to bring back both readers and subscribers to the "Mercury" was not to abuse what they liked, but to give them something they were sure to like better. Reasoning thus, Franklin began in the "Mercury" a long series of essays subscribed "The Busybody."

The first paper is taken up with some account of "The Busybody" and his purpose. He is simply Mrs. Dogood in man's clothes. He has seen with concern the growing vices and follies of his countryfolk. Reformation of these evils ought to be the concern of everybody; but what is everybody's business is nobody's business, and the business is done accordingly. The Busybody has therefore seen fit to take this nobody's business wholly into his own hands, and become a kind of *censuror morum*. Sometimes he will deliver lectures on morality or philosophy; sometimes talk on politics; sometimes, when he has nothing of his own of consequence to say, he will make use of a well-known extract from a good book, for it is the lack of good books that has made good conversation so scarce.

The second paper is against the tribe of

laughers,—gentlemen who will give themselves
an hour's diversion with the cock of a man's
hat, or the heels of his shoes, or some word
dropped unguardedly in talk; who write satires
to carry about in their pockets, and read in all
company they happen to be in; who think a
pun is wit, and judge of the strength of arguments by the strength of the lungs. In the
third was a portrait of Cretico, which Keimer
mistook for himself, and sought revenge in ridiculing the Busybody, and printing a small
tract called " A Touch of the Times. Phila.:
printed at the New Printing-Office."

Gibes Franklin could stand, but that such a
piece of typography should be thought to come
from his press was too much for him, and in
the " Mercury " of April 24, 1729, denied the
imprint. " This," said he, " may inform those
that have been induc'd to think otherwise, that
the silly paper call'd ' A Touch of the Times,'
&c., was wrote, printed and published by Mr.
Keimer ; and that his putting the words ' New
Printing-Office ' at the bottom, and instructing
the hawkers to say it was done there, is an
abuse." The new printing-office, however, did
put forth a pamphlet entitled " A Short Discourse, Proving that the Jewish or Seventh-
Day Sabbath Is Abrogated and Repealed."
And this pamphlet, there is reason to believe,

was prepared by Franklin in ridicule of Keimer, who wore the long beard, and kept the Jewish Sabbath with great strictness.

In the fourth Busybody he pretends to have had a letter begging him to pass some strictures on making long and frequent visits. The fifth he designed to be a terror to evil-doers. He has made a league with a person having the power of second sight, and is ready to show up those little crimes and vices for which the law has neither remedy nor regard, as well as those great pieces of sacred villainy so craftily done and circumspectly guarded that the law cannot take hold.

This in turn brings a letter from Titan Pleiades, astrologer. Titan has read Michael Scott, Albertus Magnus, and Cornelius Agrippa above three hundred times, in search of that wisdom which will lay before him the chests of gold and sacks of money the pirates have hidden underground. He has searched in vain, but doubts not that if the " Busybody," the second-sighted correspondent, and himself were joined, they would soon be three of the richest men in the province.

Titan was no imaginary character. One hundred and sixty years ago the belief in the existence of hidden treasure was common, and the belief unquestionably was well founded.

Some had been buried by misers, some by
thieves, and not a little by men who, having
neither stocks in which to invest nor banks in
which to deposit, hid their savings in the
earth, and dying, their secret died with them.
Even now, pots of such treasure are at times
turned up by the plow. But in Franklin's time
men were confident they could be detected
by the divining-rod and the stars. In every
colony were sharpers who for a few shillings
would furnish charms to lay the guardian spirit
and name the auspicious night, and dupes ever
ready to give the shillings and make the attempt. Day after day they would wander
through the woods watching the flight of birds,
scrutinizing the tracks of animals, turning over
bowlders, and examining the roots of trees.
The spot discovered, they would, when the
proper planets were in conjunction and the
moon was dark, hurry away with spade and
pick, toads and black-cats' fur, and, muttering
charms, panting with fatigue and trembling
with fear, dig for hours. If the east grew light
before a chest crammed with pistoles or a pot
heavy with pieces-of-eight lay before them,
they would creep home dejected but not cured.
The circle perhaps had not been truly drawn,
the charm had not been correctly said, a cloud
maybe had cut off the light of some auspicious

star. "This odd humor of digging for money, through a belief that much has been hid by pirates," the Busybody himself declared, was "mighty prevalent, insomuch that you can hardly walk half a mile out of town on any side without observing several pits dug with that design, and perhaps some lately opened."

After this essay Franklin contributed no more to the series. Of the thirty-two papers comprising "The Busybody," six are commonly ascribed to him, and the majority of the twenty-six to Joseph Breintnal. When the latter stopped writing, the purpose for which they were begun had been accomplished. Keimer, overwhelmed by disaster, was on his way to the Barbadoes. His printing-house was in the hands of David Harry; his newspaper was the property of Franklin. The whole town was reading the "Mercury," and forgetting that the "Instructor" existed. Much the same fate has overtaken "The Busybody." Franklin's six contributions are reprinted, and occasionally read. Breintnal's essays have never been collected, nor is there now living more than one man who has ever read them through.

To liken the essays of Franklin at this period of his life to those of Addison would be absurd; yet it cannot be denied that they possess merits of a rare and high order. He makes no dis-

play of ornamentation ; he indulges in no silly
flights of imagination ; he assumes no air of
learning ; he uses no figures of speech save those
the most ignorant of mankind are constantly
using unconsciously; he is free from everything
that commonly defaces the writings of young
men. Dealing with nothing but the most
homely matters, he says what he has to say
easily, simply, and in a pure English idiom. No
man ever read a sentence of Franklin's essays
and doubted what it meant. It is this simplicity and homeliness, joined to hard common sense
and wit, that gave his later writings a popularity and influence beyond those of any American
author since his day. If he has a bad habit or
a silly custom or a small vice to condemn, he
begins by presenting us with a picture of it
which we recognize at once. Then, with the
picture full before us, he draws just the moral
or passes the very censure we would do if left
to ourselves. Not a tavern-keeper but had
seen Ridentius and his followers round the fire-
place many a time. Not a merchant but knew
a Cato and a Cretico. Not a shopkeeper but
had suffered just such annoyances as Patience.

With " Busybody " number eight, Franklin
abandoned essay-writing to his friend, and all his
time and ability were given to persuading the
people on a serious question in which they and

he were deeply concerned. It was, indeed, the question of the hour, and on its decision hung the financial and commercial prosperity of the province.

Six years before, the people of Pennsylvania had, with much trepidation, ventured on the issue of a small bank of paper money : the day for its redemption was drawing near, the Lords of Trade had forbidden the issue of any more, and it seemed not unlikely that, in a little while, men would again be bartering hats for potatoes and flour for shoes because of the lack of a medium of exchange.

The earliest of the many issues of paper money in what is now the United States took place when the French and English were deeply engaged in their first struggle for the possession of Canada. James had just been driven from his throne. William and Mary had just succeeded, and the colonies, with every manifestation of delight, had taken up arms in defense of the authority of William, the Protestant religion, and the right to catch cod off the Grand Banks. For a while the war was waged with varying success. The English devastated the island of Montreal, and the French retreated from Frontenac. Then the tide turned : the French rallied, took Pemaquid, drove the English from every settlement east of Falmouth,

burned Salmon Falls, and laid Schenectady in
ashes. Driven to extremity, the English rallied, and in a congress at New York in 1690
resolved on the conquest of Canada. New
York and Connecticut were to send a land
force against Montreal. Massachusetts and Plymouth sent a fleet against Quebec. Acadia fell,
Port Royal surrendered, and New England
ruled the coast to the eastern end of Nova
Scotia. There success stopped. The command-
ers of the English troops fell to quarreling, and
the land expedition failed miserably. Frontenac, having no foe to oppose him, hurried to
Quebec, and entered the city just as the New
England fleet came sounding its way up the
St. Lawrence. The summons to surrender the
city was received with jeers. The fleet, unable
to take Quebec without the aid of the army,
sailed for Boston, to be scattered by storms
along the coast. To commemorate this signal
deliverance the French put up the Church of
our Lady of Victory. To pay the cost of the
expedition Massachusetts issued the first colonial paper money. In 1703 South Carolina followed her example.

Scarcely had King William's war ended than
Queen Anne's war broke out. Again the
French and Indians came down from Canada,
and, while Franklin was a child, laid waste the

towns of Massachusetts with fire and sword. Again the colonies sent ships and troops against Canada. Again they failed, and, to pay the cost, New Hampshire, Connecticut, Rhode Island, New York, and New Jersey imitated Massachusetts and put out bills of credit.

These early issues of credit-bills are not to be confounded with the "banks of paper money" of a later time. The amounts were small. The purpose was the payment of some pressing debt. But after the close of Queen Anne's war the belief sprang up in the minds of men that it was the duty of a government to provide a circulating medium, and that just as fast as that medium disappeared, the duty of the government was to make more. The colonists were heavy traders; the balance of trade was against them. Their specie went over to England, and, unable to practice that self-denial necessary to bring the specie back, they clamored for a currency. Then the colonies turned pawn-brokers and money-lenders, set up loan offices, and issued banks of paper money. Then whoever held a mortgage, or owned the deed of an acre of land, or was possessed of a silver tankard or a ring of gold, might, if he chose, carry it to the loan office, leave it there, and take away in exchange a number of paper bills.

In this folly Massachusetts led the way, in

1714, with a bank of fifty thousand pounds;
New York, Rhode Island, South Carolina,
quickly followed, and before seven years were
gone the loan office was established in Pennsylvania and New Jersey.

This was inevitable. The trade of New Jersey was with New York. The people of New
York had a paper currency, and paid in paper
for every cord of wood and for every boat-load
of potatoes that came over the bay. These
paper bills of New York, passing current with
the farmers of New Jersey, drove out of circulation every pistole, every carolin, every chequin,
every piece-of-eight, the bounds of the colony
contained; for the ingenuity of man never devised
and never can devise a plan for the common
circulation of specie and debased paper bills.

Thus, when 1723 came, the people of the Jerseys were paying their debts with the money
of New York, and their taxes with bits of plate,
ear-rings and finger-rings, watches, and jewelry
of every sort. Nor were coins much more plentiful in Pennsylvania. A few light pistoles, a
few pieces-of-eight, a few English shillings,
passed from hand to hand. But so far were they
from supplying the needs of trade that the men
of Chester besought the Assembly to make produce a legal tender, to prohibit the exportation
of coin, and to add one more shilling to the

Spanish dollar. The merchants of Philadelphia
and the traders of Bucks sent up petitions for
a paper currency. Most of these prayers were
heard. Another shilling was added to the dollar; produce was made a legal tender, and the
best of all forms of colonial paper money was
emitted. The bank was limited to fifteen thousand pounds; four thousand to pay the debts of
the province, and eleven thousand to be loaned
to the people. As the law distinctly stated that
the new money was to relieve the distress of
the poor, no man was suffered to borrow more
than one hundred pounds. Nor could he have
even that unless he came to the loan office and
deposited plate of three times the value, or
mortgaged lands, houses, or ground-rents of
twice the value of the sum he received, and
agreed to pay into the treasury each year five
per centum interest and one eighth the principal. So quickly were the bills taken up, and
so much were they liked, that another bank of
thirty thousand pounds was issued before the
year went out.

When the Lords of Trade heard of these
proceedings, they hastened to send back a dis-
approval and a warning. The governor was
bidden to recall the evils that had come upon
other colonies from making bills of credit. The
people were assured that nothing but tenderness

for the men in whose hands the new money was prevented the acts being laid before the king for repeal. A warning was given that, should any more acts emitting paper money be passed, they would surely be disallowed. On the first of March, 1731, the bills were to become irredeemable, and as that day came nearer and nearer the merchants and traders grew more and more uneasy, and more and more doubtful what to do. The opponents of paper money dwelt much on the danger of such a currency and the threat of the Lords of Trade. The friends of paper money had much to say of the brisk times that followed the issues of 1723.

But the arguments that prevailed most, the arguments that brought over the doubting, that persuaded the governor and the assembly, in open defiance of the orders from England, not only to reissue the old money, but to put out thirty thousand pounds of new, were contained in a little pamphlet from the pen of Franklin, entitled "A Modest Inquiry into the Nature and Necessity of a Paper Currency."

"There is," he begins by saying, "a certain quantity of money needed to carry on trade. More than this sum can be productive of no real use. Less than this quantity is always productive of serious evils. Lack of money in a country puts up the rate of interest, and puts down the price of that part of produce used in trade. It keeps skilled workmen from coming in; it induces many already in to go out; it causes, in a country like America, a far greater use of English goods than there otherwise would be. These facts being understood, it is easy [he asserts] to see what kind of men will, in the face of these facts, be for, and what kind of men will be against, a further issue of paper bills. On the side of the enemies to the bills will be the lawyers, the money-lenders, the speculators in land, and the men who, in any way, are dependent upon them. On the side of the friends to the issue of bills will be the lovers of trade, the supporters of manufactures, and the men who have the interest of the proprietors of the province truly at heart.

"The enemies to paper money cry out, that, if any more be issued, the value of the whole of it will sink." This suggests an inquiry into the nature of money in general, and bills of credit in particular. Money, he declares, "is a medium of exchange; and whatever men agree to make the medium is, to those who have it, the very things they want, because it will buy for them the very things they want. It is cloth to him who wants cloth. It is corn to him who wants corn. Custom has made gold and silver the materials for this medium of exchange. But the measure of value for this medium is not gold and silver, but labor. Labor is as much a measure of the value of silver as of anything else. Suppose one man employed to raise corn, while another man is busy refining gold. At the end of a year the complete produce of corn and the complete produce of silver are the natural price of each other. If the one be twenty bushels and the other twenty ounces, then one ounce of silver is worth the labor of raising one bushel of corn. Money therefore, as bullion, is valuable by so much labor as it costs to produce that bullion.

"But this bullion, when coined into money, is heavy, consumes time in the counting, cannot be easily hidden. Hence it is that at Hamburgh, at Amsterdam, at London, at Venice, the centers of vast trade, men have resorted, for sake of convenience, to banks of deposit and bills of credit. Into the banks they put their gold and silver, and take out bills to the value of what they put in. Thus the money of the country is doubled, the banks loaning out the gold at interest, the people making their great payments in bills.

"As the men of Europe put in money for the security of the bills, so [says he] men in

Pennsylvania, not having money, pledge their land."

These principles stated, Franklin proceeds to consider which kind of security is the better, — whether bills issued on money or bills issued on land are more likely to fall in value. His answer is, of course, bills issued on money. " Gold and silver may become so plentiful that a coin which at one time purchased the labor of a man for twenty days, will not at another time purchase that same man's labor for fifteen days. Every credit bill issued on that coin as security must therefore depreciate." And this he claims is precisely what has taken place in Europe ever since the discovery of gold in America. " But in Pennsylvania the people are rapidly increasing, land is always in demand, its value is always rising, and bills of credit issued on it as security must of necessity grow more and more valuable every day."

That Franklin was deceived by such shallow arguments, that he really meant what he said, is difficult to believe. He has come down to us as the great teacher of thrift, of frugality, of fair and honest dealing. Yet man cannot devise anything more at variance with these virtues than paper money. It promotes speculation; it encourages extravagance; every piece of it is a symbol of fraud. The value stamped upon its face is one thing; the real value is another thing. But Franklin was now a partisan, and was soon rewarded for his partisanship. Had he meddled in theology, had he written a pamphlet on the Keithian schism, the presses of Andrew Bradford and David Harry would have teemed with replies. But he wrote on a question of political economy. Not a man among the supporters of specie money could reply, and his remarks were hailed as unanswerable. When, therefore, his friends carried the day, and thirty thousand pounds in paper money was ordered to be printed, Benjamin Franklin was made the printer. "A very profitable job," says he in the Autobiography, "and a great help to me."

Bad as were his notions of political economy, his pamphlet contained one great truth, — the truth that labor is a measure of value. Whether he discovered, or, as is not unlikely, borrowed it, he was the first to openly assert it; and his it remained till, forty-seven years later, Adam Smith adopted and reaffirmed it in "The Wealth of Nations."

CHAPTER III.

1729–1748.

THE pamphlet on paper money finished,
Franklin wrote nothing for six months. By
that time Keimer had fallen deeply in debt, had
been dragged to jail for the ninth time, had
compounded with his creditors, had been liber-
ated, had failed again, and had sold his newspaper to Franklin & Meredith for a trifle.
Ninety subscribers then took the "Instructor"
each week, and thirty-nine weekly numbers had
been issued. With the fortieth, which bears
date October 2, 1729, a new era opened. The
silly name was cut down to "The Pennsylvania Gazette." The Quaker nomenclature
was dropped, "The Religious Courtship" ceased
to be published. Except at long intervals, no
extracts from Chambers's Dictionary appeared;
and, for the first time in the history of our
country, a newspaper was issued twice a week.
In this Franklin was far, indeed too far, in
advance of the age, and, when the bad weather
came and the postrider made his trips northward

but once a fortnight, the "Gazette" once more became a weekly paper, and remained so for years.

Thus stripped of nonsense, the "Gazette" began to be conducted on strictly business principles. Franklin knew that to make it profitable he must have advertisements, that to secure advertisements he must have circulation, and that to get circulation he must have buyers out of town. But to get out-of-town subscribers was no easy matter. Newspapers were not mailable. The postriders, therefore, could not be forced to take the "Gazette," and Bradford, who was postmaster, would not allow them to take it voluntarily. They were accordingly bribed in secret to smuggle the "Gazettes" into their postbags, and do their best to secure subscriptions.

To get a circulation in Philadelphia Franklin resorted to clever expedients. He strove to make the "Gazette" amuse its readers, and to persuade the readers to write for the "Gazette;" for he well knew that every contributor would buy a dozen copies of the paper containing his piece from sheer love of seeing himself in print.

In the first number published under his name this invitation is very modestly given. He knew it was a common belief that the author of a newspaper should be a man well versed in languages, in geography, in history; be able to speak of wars, both by land and sea; be familiar with the interests of princes and states, the secrets of courts, the manners and customs of all nations; have a ready pen, and be able to narrate events clearly, intelligently, and in a few words. But such men were scarce in these remote parts of the world, and the printer therefore must hope to make up among his friends what was wanting in himself. And this invitation is repeated again and again. Assurances are given that a series of papers on "Speculation" and "Amusement" are shortly to be published, and gentlemen "disposed to try their hands in some little performance" are urged to make use of this chance. No gentlemen were disposed to try their hands, and the papers never appeared. Some essays on "Primitive Christianity" did appear, and, having offended the orthodox, they are urged to inform the public what is the truth.

There is no reason to suppose that such appeals produced a single essay. But the pretense that they did is well kept up, and for many years the editor carried on a lively correspondence with himself. He starts a question of casuistry in one number, and answers it in the next. He suggests and discusses reforms and improvements in long communications beginning, " Mr. Printer," and, when the town is dull, has a letter from Alice Addertongue, or a note from Bob Brief, or a piece of pleasantry just coarse enough to excite a laugh. Now he pretends that he is besought to —

" Pray let the prettiest creature in this place know (by publishing this) that if it was not for her affectation she would be absolutely irresistible ; " and, of course, in the next issue of the " Gazette " has six denials from the six prettiest creatures in the place. He hears that in Bucks County a flash of lightning melted the pewter button off the waistband of a farmer's breeches, and observes, " 'T is well nothing else thereabouts was made of pewter." Another week the casuist offers an " honorary reward to any cabalist " who shall demonstrate that Z contains more occult virtue than X. Then there is " a pecuniary gratification " for anybody who shall prove " that a man's having a Property in a tract of land, more or less, is thereby entitled to any advantage, irrespective of understanding, over another Fellow, who has no other Estate than the air to breathe in, the Earth to walk upon, and all the rivers of the world to drink of." When nothing else will serve, his own mishaps are described for the amusement of the town. " Thursday last, a certain P——r ('t is not customary to give names at length on these occasions) walking carefully in clean Clothes over some Barrels of Tar on Carpenter's Wharff, the head of one of them unluckily gave way, and let a Leg of him in above the Knee. Whether he was upon the Catch at that time, we cannot say, but 't is certain he caught a *Tar-tar*. 'T was observed he sprang out again right briskly, verifying the common saying, As nimble as a Bee in a Tarbarrel. You must know there are several sorts of Bees: 't is true he was no Honey Bee, nor yet a Humble Bee; but a Boo-Bee he may be allowed to be, namely B. F."

His more serious contributions to the "Gazette" may be classed as dialogues, as bad as those of any writer; pieces of domestic and political economy after the manner of "Poor Richard;" moral essays and pieces of pleasantry and mirth, which he has himself declared "have a secret charm in them to allay the heats and tumours of our spirits, and to make a man forget his restless resentments."

Writings of this description would usually appear when storms delayed the London packets and the "Craftsman" and the "British Journal" failed to come to hand; when winter interrupted travel, and the postman made his trips northward but once a fortnight; when the freezing of the rivers shut out the coasters, and news grew scarce and trade grew dull; when the town, no longer absorbed in business, was more than ever ready to be amused. Anything to break the dullness was acceptable, and something was sure to come. One week he affects to be one of the tribe of pedants whose business it is to expurgate, annotate, and deface the text of ancient authors with silly comments and with useless notes; takes a nursery rhyme for his text; has much to say of readings, manuscripts, and versions; and treats his readers to a good satire, which has, in our day, found an unconscious imitator in the author of the sermon on "Old Mother Hubbard." Another week he is a purchaser laughing at the tradesmen for always protesting that they sell wares for less than cost; and in the next number is a tradesman laughing at buyers who assert in every shop they enter that the goods they are examining can be had for less elsewhere. But better than any of these are "The Meditations on a Quart Mug," the account of the witch trial at Mount Holly, and the "Speech of Miss Polly Baker before a Court of Judicatory in New England, where she was presented for the fifth time for having a Bastard Child."

To a generation that frowns on Tom Jones and Peregrine Pickle, the speech of Miss Polly is coarse in the extreme. But it enjoyed in its own time an immense popularity, was printed and reprinted for fifty years, was cited by Abbé Raynal in his " Histoire Philosophique des Deux Indes " as a veritable fact, and is assuredly a rare piece of wit. The account of the witch - ducking is nearly as witty, cannot be accused of being coarse, is not to be found among Franklin's collected writings, and may therefore be given in full.

" Saturday last, at Mount Holly, about eight miles from this place [Burlington], near three hundred people were gathered together to see an experiment or two tried on some persons accused of witchcraft. It seems the accused had been charged with making the neighbours' sheep dance in an uncommon manner, and with causing hogs to speak and sing Psalms, etc., to the great terror and amazement of the king's good and peaceful subjects in the province ; and the accusers, being very positive that if the accused were weighed against a Bible, the Bible would prove too heavy for them ; or that, if they were bound and put into the River they would swim ; the said accused, desirous to make innocence appear, voluntarily offered to undergo the said trials if two of the most violent of their accusers would be tried with them. Accordingly the time and place was agreed on and advertised

about the country. The accused were one man
and one woman: and the accusers the same.
The parties being met and the people got together, a grand consultation was held before
they proceeded to trial, in which it was agreed
to use the scales first; and a committee of men
were appointed to search the man, and a committee of women to search the woman, to see if
they had anything of weight about them, particularly pins.   After the scrutiny was over a
huge great Bible belonging to the Justice of the
Peace was produced, and a lane through the
populace was made from the Justice's house to
the scales, which were fixed on a gallows erected
for that purpose opposite to the house, that the
Justice's wife and the rest of the ladies might
see the trial without coming among the mob,
and after the manner of Moorefield a large ring
was also made.   Then came out of the house a
grave, tall man carrying the Holy Writ before
the wizard as solemnly as the sword-bearer of
London before the Lord Mayor. The wizard
was first placed in the scale, and over him was
read a chapter out of the Book of Moses, and
then the Bible was put in the other scale, which,
being kept down before, was immediately let
go; but, to the great surprise of the spectators,
flesh and blood came down plump and out-
weighed that great good Book by abundance.

After the same manner the others were served,
and the lumps of mortality severally were too
heavy for Moses and all the Prophets and Apos-
tles. This being over, the accusers and the
rest of the mob, not being satisfied with the experiment, would have trial by water. Accordingly a most solemn procession was made to the
mill-pond, where the accused and accusers, being stripped (saving only to the women their
shifts) were bound hand and foot and severally
placed in the water, lengthways, from the side
of a barge or Flat, having for security only a
rope about the middle of each, which was held
by some one in the Flat. The accuser man
being thin and spare with some difficulty began
to sink at last; but the rest, every one of them,
swam very light upon the water. A sailor in
the Flat jumped out upon the back of the man
accuser thinking to drive him down to the bottom; but the person bound, without any help,
came up some time before the other. The woman accuser being told that she did not sink,
would be ducked a second time; when she swam
again as light as before. Upon which she declared that the accused had bewitched her to
make her so light, and that she would be ducked
again a hundred times but that she would duck
the Devil out of her. The accused man, being
surprised at his own swimming, was not so con-

fident of his own innocence as before, but said, 'If I am a witch, it is more than I know.' The more thinking part of the spectators were of opinion that any person so bound and placed in the water (unless they were mere skin and bones) would swim till their breath was gone, and their lungs filled with water. But it being the general belief of the populace that the women's shifts and the garters with which they were bound helped to support them, it is said they are to be tried again the next warm weather, naked."

This readiness of Franklin to provoke laughter sometimes cost him dear. Thus it happened on one occasion that he was called on to print a notice setting forth that a certain ship would, on a certain day, sail for a certain port in the Barbadoes, and that freighters and passengers might make terms with the captain on the wharf. He made of the notice just such a hand bill as it was then the custom to fasten on the walls of the coffee-houses and the taverns, and, to insure the bill being read, added these words of his own: " N. B. No Sea Hens, nor Black Gowns, will be admitted on any terms." The end was at once attained. No one who read the notice but went straightway and brought some one else to read it, and in a few days the whole town was laughing at the Black Gowns, and asking what a Sea Hen could be.

But the Black Gowns saw nothing to laugh at; took offense, and sent Franklin notice that as a punishment for his maliciousness they not only would cease buying his " Gazette," but would use their best endeavors to prevent others from buying.

Franklin kept his temper and replied. He was, he said, so often censured by people for printing things they thought ought not to be printed, that he was strongly tempted to write a standing apology and publish it once a year. These faultfinders forgot the difference between the printing trade and any other trade. A table constructed by a Jew, a pair of shoes made by an infidel, a piece of ironmongery beaten out by a heretic, give no offense to the most orthodox. But a printer had to do with men's opinions. Opinions were as various as faces, and it was therefore impossible to get a living by printing without offending some one, or perhaps many. It was unreasonable for any man, or any set of men, to expect to be pleased with everything put in type. It was unreasonable to suppose that printers approved of everything they put in type, or to insist that they should print only what they did approve. If they sometimes put forth vicious and silly things not worth reading, they did so, not because they liked such things themselves, but because the people were so viciously educated that good things were not encouraged. A small impression of The Psalms of David had been upon his shelves for above two years: yet he had known a large impression of Robin Hood's Songs to go off in a twelvemonth. As for the hand bill that caused so much offense, he printed it, not because he hated the clergy, nor because he despised religion, but because he got five shillings by printing it, which was just five shillings more than anybody would have given him to let it alone. When he considered the variety of humors among men, he despaired of pleasing everybody. Yet he should not on that account leave off printing. He should go on with the business; he should not burn his press nor melt his type.

When he again offended and was called to an account, the reply was very different. A barber, hair-dresser, and peruke-maker who had long been advertising in the " Gazette" suddenly informed the public that he would no longer shave and cut hair. News being scarce and the taverns dull, Franklin took the notice for a text, printed it at the head of an essay on shavers and trimmers in business, in politics, and in the church, and heard from every advertiser in his newspaper. If this thing went on, he was given to understand, there would soon be an end to all advertising. What guaranty had they that the next merchant who advertised Jamaica rum or very good sack would not see his notice at the head of a long disquisition on Drunkards and the Evils of Drink?

To these protests Franklin replied : —

"My paper on 'Shavers and Trimmers' in the last 'Gazette' being generally condemned, I at first imputed it to the want of Taste and Relish for pieces of that Force and Beauty which none but thoroughly-bred Gentlemen can produce. But upon advice of Friends, whose judgement I could depend on, I examined myself, and to my shame must confess that I found myself to be an uncircumcised Jew, whose Excrescences of Hair, Nails, Flesh, &c., did burthen and disgrace my Natural Endowments ; but having my Hair and Nails since lopp'd off and shorn, and my fleshy Excrescences circumcised, I now appear in my wonted Lustre and expect speedy admission among the Levites, which I have already the honor of among the Poets and Natural Philosophers. I have one thing more to say, which is, that I had no real animosity against the person whose advertisement I made the matter of my paper."

Among the papers on domestic economy, the complaint of Anthony Afterwit, who has been hurried from one piece of extravagance to

another by a foolish wife; the reply of Patience
Teacroft defending the wife; the letter of Celia
Single on the idleness and extravagance of men,
are decidedly the best productions. Franklin
was a born moralist. When a lad of twenty
he wrote a letter to his sister, a girl of fifteen,
on the duties of a housewife, which in its kind
is inimitable. It was quite in his natural vein.
But the moment he quitted this natural vein
and undertook compositions of another sort, he
began to utter the stale sayings of the schoolboy and the preacher. His remarks on the
" Usefulness of Mathematics," on " Government," on " How to Please in Conversation; "
his dialogues between Philocles and Horatius,
between Socrates and Critico, between Socrates
and Glaucon, between two Presbyterians on
staying away from church, in which the behavior of Mr. Hemphill is warmly defended,—
are not worth reading. The pieces called " The
Family of the Boxes " and " The Drinkers' Dictionary," are positively foolish. On the other
hand, " The Meditations on a Quart Mug," and
the " Thoughts of the Ephemera on Human
Vanity," which he afterwards rewrote for
Madame Brillon, could not have been done better by Addison himself.

Below these, and much below, are the essays
against swearing, " On Lying Tradesmen," " On

Scandal," " On the Waste of Life," " On True Happiness," " On the Rules and Maxims for Promoting Matrimonial Happiness." Mingled with these are pieces of a very different kind,— pieces whose purpose is either to bring about some needed reform, or strongly affect public opinion. One of his earliest attempts at this sort of writing was in 1735, when he became for a time embroiled in a dispute with the Presbyterian ministers. The cause of the trouble was Samuel Hemphill, a young Presbyterian preacher, who came from the north of Ireland. Hemphill had been licensed by the Presbytery of Strabane, had been tried for heresy, had been acquitted, had come over to America, and had been followed by a letter from one of his old foes. The letter set forth that Mr. Hemphill was a Deist, a New-Light man, or a heretic of some sort, and ought not to be suffered to have a place in the true fold. The busybody to whom it was sent carried it to the minister, read it to all who would listen, and Mr. Hemphill was soon before the presbytery of New Castle. He was again acquitted, and came to Philadelphia, where Jedidiah Andrews, who preached in the old Buttonwood Church, gave up the pulpit to him once each Sunday. Young, eloquent, with a good delivery and an easy flow of words, he drew crowds to hear, and of those who listened none liked him better than Franklin.

Andrews meanwhile grew jealous, and went among the congregation calling Hemphill a Deist, a Socinian, a missionary sent from Ireland to corrupt the faith once delivered to the saints, and soon had him before a commission of the synod. There Andrews accused him of saying and doing dreadful things. So depraved was Hemphill that, when he prayed, he prayed not for any church, nor for any minister, but for all mankind. In summing up the distempers of the soul, he said nothing of the distemper by original sin. He had been heard to say that reason is our rule, and was given for a rule. He had spoken against the need of spiritual pangs in order to conversion. The commission, to their great grief, found him guilty and suspended him. Thereupon Franklin took up his cause, and wrote in his defence two pamphlets and two pieces in the " Gazette." One of the pieces was called " A Dialogue between two Presbyterians on Staying Away from Church." The other, which soon appeared as a pamphlet, was called " A Letter to a Friend in the Country Containing the Substance of a Sermon preach'd at Philadelphia, in the Congregation of the Rev. Mr. Hemphill." A third, and the strongest of them all, is " Some Observations on the

Proceedings against the Rev. Mr. Hemphill;
with a Vindication of his Sermons." It was
eagerly read, passed rapidly through two editions, and quickly led to a violent pamphlet
war. One writer answered the "Letter to a
Friend" in a pamphlet of thirty-two pages.
Another, or perhaps the same, attacked the
"Observations" in a yet longer pamphlet entitled "A Vindication of the Reverend Commission of the Synod," and was in turn promptly
answered by Franklin. He called his pamphlet "A Defense of the Rev. Mr. Hemphill's
Observations," gave a sketch of Mr. Hemphill's
history, took up the charges preferred by Mr.
Andrews, examined them carefully, went over
the finding of the reverend commission, accused
it of acting after the manner and with the spirit
of the Spanish Inquisition, and provoked a reply
most ruinous to his cause. The title was, "Remarks upon the Defense," and the author declared Mr. Hemphill to be a reverend plagiary,
and made good the charge. One of his sermons
he had taken from Dr. Clarke, an open Arian.
Three more were the work of Dr. Ibbots, who
assisted Dr. Clarke. Yet another was taken
from a published sermon of Dr. Forster. Hemphill afterwards owned to Franklin that each of
his sermons was the work of some one else.
But even then his defender flinched not, and

stoutly declared that he would far rather hear a good though borrowed sermon, than a sermon that was original and bad.

When Franklin wrote his Autobiography, he did not believe a copy of one of his pamphlets to be extant. Sparks, when editing the doctor's works, asserted that none of them had ever been found. Both were mistaken. Copies of each of the pamphlets are in existence, and have, within quite recent years, been sold at the auction block.

Franklin next took up the matter of reform. Whenever he had such work to do, it was his custom to write a paper with great care on the abuse to be corrected, and read it some evening to the Junto. If the Junto thought well of it, he would put "Mr. Franklin," or "To the Printer," at the top, and "Philadelphus," or "Old Tradesman," at the bottom, and publish it in the "Gazette." An answer or two, likewise written by Franklin, would follow, and in a few weeks the city council, or the grand jury, or the assembly, would have the matter in charge.

It was by such means that he reformed the city watch; that he established the fire companies; that he persuaded the people to light the streets, to sweep the pavements around the market, and to organize the first militia. On the 1st of July, 1700, when the city was still a little place, the governor and council established the watch. The watch consisted of one good and trusty man, who each night went the rounds of the city, rang a small bell, cried the hours, described the weather, and roused the constable if he spied a chimney burning, or met a drunken Indian on the streets. Five years later, when the city was thought a great one and ten wards were established, the constable of each in turn was commanded to summon every day nine citizens, who, with himself, should constitute the watch for his ward.

The duty of these ten men has been clearly laid down in a charge which, for absurdity, is surpassed by that of Dogberry alone. But nothing in the charge made the watch as worthless as the conduct of the citizens themselves. Six shillings paid to the constable would secure exemption from his warning for a year ; and that man was poor indeed who could not get together six shillings to be free of such service. The band, therefore, that went with the constable on his nightly rounds, came in time to be made up of the very scum of the town. They passed whole nights in the tippling houses ; they often ceased to walk their rounds, and, when they did, to meet them was more to be dreaded than meeting a thief. To end this abuse, Franklin proposed a permanent, well-paid watch; addressed himself first to the Junto, and then to the people, who addressed and petitioned the assembly for eight years before the reform was made.

His suggestions for the better extinguishing of fires were more speedily adopted. For the prevention of fires the law prescribed in what kind of ovens bakers should bake bread, in what kind of shops coopers should make casks; fined any man who smoked on the streets of the built part of the city, or suffered his sooty chimney to burst into flame; and compelled captains of ships moored at the wharf to put out all fires when the clock struck eight, unless the mayor gave a license to keep them burning. For extinguishing fires, each householder kept in his shop or his pantry a bucket and a fourteen-foot swab; while the city provided hooks, ladders, and three rude engines of English make. At the first cry of fire the whole town was in excitement; the laborer quit his work, the apprentice dropped his tools, buyers and sellers swarmed from the market; and the shopkeeper, calling his wife to watch his goods, seized his bucket and hurried away. About the burning building all was confusion and disorder. No man was in authority. Each man did as he pleased. Some fell into line and helped to pass the full buckets

from the pump to the engine, or the empty
buckets from the engine to the pump; some
caught up the hooks and pulled down blazing
boards and shingles; some rushed into the building with their ozenbrig bags, and came out laden with household stuff.

All this energy, excellent as it was, seemed
to Franklin misused. If so much could be done
in a way so bad, a hundred-fold more, he
thought, could be done if a little order were
introduced. Thinking so, he wrote two papers
on the subject of fires, read them to the Junto,
and published them in the "Gazette." The
matter is in no wise remarkable; but the style
is a good specimen of persuasive argument.
That they had this effect on people in general
is doubtful; but they did on the Junto, who
quickly formed the Union Fire Company, the
first of its kind in the province. Others followed their example, and to the "Union,"
"The Hand-in-hand" and "The Heart-in-
hand" were soon added.

Yet another of his pieces in the "Gazette"
must not be passed over in silence. It is in
verse, and is a paraphrase of the sublime lamentation of David over the death of Jonathan and
Saul. He begins by stating his belief that the
art of poetry was made known to the Hebrews
by Moses; gives reasons for thinking so; takes

up the lamentation, and observes that it has many times been paraphrased in English, that none of the paraphrases are quite to his mind, and that he will therefore give the reader one of his own make, as bad perhaps as any of them. The poem is long; but a few stanzas will serve as a specimen of all: —

I.

Unhappy Day! distressing sight,
Israel, the Land of Heaven's delight,
How is thy strength, thy beauty fled!
On the high places of the fight,
Behold thy Princes fall'n, thy Sons of Victory dead.

II.

Ne'er be it told in Gath, nor known
Among the streets of Askelon;
How will Philista's youth rejoice
 And triumph in thy shame,
And girls with weak unhallow'd voice
Chant the dishonors of the Hebrew name!

III.

Mountains of Gilboa, let no dew
Nor fruitful shower descend on you;
Curse on your fields thro' all the year!
No flow'ry blessing there appear,
Nor golden ranks of harvest stand
To grace the altar, nor to seed the land.
  'T was on those inauspicious fields
  Judean heroes lost their shields.
'T was there (ah, base reproach and scandal of the day!)
  Thy shield, O Saul! was cast away,
As tho' the Prophet's horn had never shed
  Its sacred odors on thy head.

Many years later, when age and experience should have taught him better, he again made a paraphrase of a chapter of Job. In no book, it is safe to say, is the force and beauty of the English tongue so finely shown as in King James's Bible. But on Franklin that force and beauty were wholly lost. The language he pronounced obsolete. The style he thought not agreeable, and he was for a new rendering in which the turn of phrase and manner of expression should be modern. That there might be no mistake as to his meaning, he gave a sample of how the work should be done ; took some verses from the first chapter of Job, stripped them of every particle of grace, beauty, imagery, terseness, and strength, and wrote a paraphrase which, of all paraphrases of the Bible, is surely the worst.

JOB.	FRANKLIN.
Verse 6. Now there was a day when the sons of God came to present themselves before the Lord, and Satan came also amongst them.	Verse 6. And it being levee day in Heaven, all God's nobility came to court to present themselves before him ; and Satan also appeared in the circle, as one of the ministry.
7. And the Lord said unto Satan, Whence comest thou ? Then Satan answered the Lord and said, From going	7. And God said unto Satan, You have been some time absent ; where were you ? And Satan answered,

to and fro in the earth, and from walking up and down in it.

8. And the Lord said unto Satan, Hast thou considered my servant Job, that there is none like him in the earth, a perfect and an upright man, one that feareth God and escheweth evil?

9. And Satan answered the Lord and said, Doth Job fear God for naught?

. . . .

11. But put forth thine hand now, and touch all that he hath, and he will curse thee to thy face.

I have been at my country-seat, and in different places visiting my friends.

8. And God said, Well, what think you of Lord Job? You see he is my best friend, a perfectly honest man, full of respect for me, and avoiding every thing that might offend me.

9. And Satan answered, Does your majesty imagine that his good conduct is the effect of personal attachment and affection?

. . . .

11. Try him — only withdraw your favor, turn him out of his places, and withhold his pensions, and you will soon find him in the opposition.

The plan is beneath criticism. Were such a piece of folly ever begun, there would remain but one other depth of folly to which it would be possible to go down. Franklin proposed to fit out the Kingdom of Heaven with lords, nobles, a ministry, and levee days. It would on the same principle be proper to make another version suitable for republics; a version from which every term and expression peculiar to a monarchy should be carefully kept out, and only such as are applicable to a republic put in. Nor would he have hesitated to make such a version. The Bible was to him in no sense a book for spiritual guidance. It showed a most amazing knowledge of the heart of man, of the actions of men, of the passions and temptations of men, and of the way in which during moments of passion and temptation men would surely act. It abounded in examples as often to be shunned as followed. It taught just such lessons as he was teaching, — lessons of honesty, thrift, diligence, worldly wisdom, and sometimes of politics. But it displayed this knowledge, held up these examples, and taught these lessons, that men might be happier, not in another world, but in this.

Hence it was that the first chapter of Job taught him nothing but a lesson in politics. In a piece called "The Levee," and still placed among the bagatelles, Franklin set forth his understanding of the strange scene, and asks what instruction is to be gathered from it. His answer is ready: "Trust not a single person with the government of your state. For if the Deity himself, being the monarch, may for a time give way to calumny, and suffer it to operate the destruction of the best of subjects, what mischief may you not expect from such power in a mere man, though the best of men, from whom the truth is often industriously hidden, and to whom falsehood is often presented in its place by artful, interested, and malicious courtiers?"

Distasteful as the language of Scripture was to Franklin, he nevertheless wrote two pieces in close imitation. The first he called "A Parable Against Persecution," printed it in the same way Bibles are printed, and fastened it in his own copy at the end of Genesis as the fifty-first chapter of that book. His custom then was, on some evening when a host of friends were seated about him, to lead the talk to the subject of parables, bring out his Bible, read the pretended chapter of Genesis, and listen with delight while his guests one by one declared they had never heard the parable before, nor knew such a chapter of Genesis existed.

In this way Lord Kames saw it, and in 1774 reprinted the parable in his "Sketches of the History of Man." Thence it passed to Vaughan's edition of Franklin's works, and so to volume 50 of the Gentleman's Magazine, where a lively dispute soon took place over the question who wrote it. An admirer of Jeremy Taylor informed Mr. Urban that Franklin had taken the parable bodily from Taylor's "Polemical Discourses," where it could be found at the end of the twenty-second section of "The Liberty of Prophesying." This was true, and the curious began at once to ask where Taylor got it; for he headed the parable with the words, "I end with a story which I find in the Jews' Books." At last a writer in the Repository for May, 1788, announced that he had found the "Jews' Book," that it had been published at Amsterdam in 1651, had been translated by George Gentius, and that in the dedication was the parable, ascribed to the Persian poet Saadi. Lord Teignmouth now translated the version of Saadi, and sent it to Bishop Heber, who put it among the notes to his "Life of Jeremy Taylor." Franklin meanwhile was warmly defended in the Repository for June, 1788, and declared, in a letter to Mr. Vaughan, that the Scripture language and the two verses at the end were all he could claim as his own. But the discussion as to where he got it was still going on in the Gentleman's Magazine as late as 1791. In 1794 the Parable was printed at London in the form of a tract, and sold for a halfpenny.

The second parable is on brotherly love. Some Midian merchants passing by with camels bearing spices, myrrh, and iron-ware, Reuben buys an axe. There is none other in his father's house, and Simeon, Levi, and Judah come in turn to borrow it. But Reuben will not lend, and the brothers are forced to send after the Ishmaelite merchants and buy each of them an axe for himself. Now it happens, as Reuben hews timber on the river-bank, his axe falls into the water. Unable to find it, he goes in turn to his brothers to borrow. Simeon refuses. Levi consents, but consents so grudgingly that Reuben will not borrow; whereupon Judah seeing his distress, hastens to him and offers the axe unasked.

Each of these pieces was much admired, and the fame of them involved Franklin in a work that signally failed. Sir Francis Dashwood was then busy abridging the Book of Common Prayer. Lord Le Despencer asked Franklin to help. He did so, wrote the preface, cut down the catechism, and paraphrased the Psalms. This new catechism consisted of two questions: What is your duty to God? and What is your duty to your neighbor? The new Psalms were what was left of the old ones when repetitions and imprecations had been taken out. Poetry had no charms for him. He seldom read any. He never wrote any. The most that can be said of his verses is, that for so matter-of-fact a man some of them are very good.

Of doggerel he has left plenty. The lines that stand at the heads of the monthly calendars in " Poor Richard " are his. There is more of the same kind in the Gazette. But of good verse, not six pieces are extant. The Lines on Paper; the Drinking Song for the Junto, beginning " Fair Venus calls ; " " My Plain Country Joan ; " " David's Lamentation," and a humorous poem never published, make up the list. The unpublished piece is among his papers in the State Department at Washington.

After 1740, Franklin almost ceased to contribute essays to the Gazette. In 1748 he sold it, with his printing-house, to his partner David Hall. As a newspaper there is little to be said in its behalf. The printing is well done, for, as a printer, the colonies did not produce his equal. But as an editor, he was outdone, and much outdone, by William Bradford of the Journal. It seemed impossible for him to rise above the job-printer. The years during which the printing-house and the Gazette were under his control were years of great literary activity. During these years the press of Pennsylvania showed a boldness and fertility to which the press of no other colony approached. The classics were translated, magazines were begun, newspapers in foreign languages established,

German type introduced, and the largest work printed before the Revolution issued. From the Pennsylvania press came, before 1748, " Epictetus his Morals," the first translation of a classic issued in America ; " Philadelphische Zeitung," the first German newspaper ; and " Zionitischer Weyrauch-Hügel," the first book printed from German type ; the first and second monthly magazine, and the first bible published in a European tongue. Nor did enterprise end here. In 1764 came forth the first religious periodical, and in 1785 the first daily newspaper in North America. Yet for all this activity we owe nothing or next to nothing to Franklin. The encouragement he gave to letters was not by printing good books, but by putting it in the power of his poorer townsmen to read them.

To bring this about he founded the Philadelphia Library. The idea was not a sudden one. When a lad of one-and-twenty, in Keimer's employ, he formed his boon companions into the famous Junto. The number was limited to twelve, and no one could be a member till he had, with his hand upon his heart, declared that he loved mankind ; that he thought no man ought to be harmed in body, name, or goods because of the opinions he held or the creed he followed ; that he loved truth for the sake of truth, should seek diligently for it, and when found make it known to others. On Friday evenings, when the Junto met, it was usual to read through a list of questions, which each one present must answer if he could, and to bring up some matter for general debate. The debates and the questions often made it necessary to bring a book, and noticing this, Franklin proposed that each should bring all the books he owned and leave them in the room of the Junto for the good of all. This was done. But when a year was gone, some of the members finding their books had been badly treated, took them away. Even for this Franklin had an expedient ready, and suggested that fifty subscribers be found who were willing to pay forty shillings down, and ten shillings a year thereafter for maintaining a library. The suggestion seemed a good one, and the members of the Junto were soon carrying round papers to which subscribers set their names but slowly. Five months were spent in filling the list, four more went by before the shillings were collected. But at last, in March, 1732, forty-five pounds were sent to London to be laid out in the purchase of books. In October the first invoice arrived, and the Library was opened in the room where the Junto met.

CHAPTER IV.

1732–1748.

WHEN the year 1732 opened, Franklin's career of prosperity may be said to have begun. He had ended his partnership with Meredith, had paid his debts, had married a wife, set up a newspaper, and opened a shop, which defies description, hard by the market-place in High Street. There were to be had imported books, legal blanks, paper and parchment, Dutch quills and Aleppo ink, perfumed soap, Rhode Island cheese, chapbooks such as the peddlers hawked, pamphlets such as the Quakers read, live-geese feathers, bohea tea, coffee, very good sack, and cash for old rags. Everything connected with this miscellaneous business was carried on in strict accordance with the maxims of Poor Richard. No idle servant fattened in his house. His wife, in such moments as could be snatched from the kitchen and the tub, folded newspapers, stitched pamphlets, and sold inkhorns and pocket-books, which, as paper-money drove out the coin, came more and more into use.

Franklin meanwhile managed the printing-house, made lampblack, cast type, made rude cuts for the paper-money bills, and might be seen at times trundling home a wheelbarrow loaded with paper bought at some neighboring merchant's shop.

Industrious, thrifty, saving, full of hard common sense and worldly wisdom, he suffered no chance to pass unused, and rose rapidly to the place of chief printer in the province. The business of the place in a year would not now suffice to keep a journeyman printer occupied three months. Never since the press had been set up in Pennsylvania had all the issues in any one year numbered thirty. In 1732 they were but nineteen; but of the nineteen, three, bearing the imprint of Franklin, are noteworthy. One was " Philadelphische Zeitung," the first German newspaper printed in America. Another was " The Honour of the Gout," a book that long afterwards suggested the famous Dialogue between Franklin and the Gout. The third was the greatest of all almanacs — " Poor Richard."

The publication of " Poor Richard " he was tempted to undertake by the quick and great returns such pamphlets were sure to bring in. For the mere copy of popular almanacs, printers were then compelled to pay down in advance

from twenty to thirty pounds each year; no
mean sum at a time when the chief justice
was given but one hundred pounds a year, when
the associate justice got but fifty pounds, and
when the attorney-general was forced to be
content with sixty.

Such prices could well afford to be paid, for
the almanac was the one piece of literature of
which the sale was sure. Not a household for
a hundred miles around the printer but, if there
was sixpence to spare, would have a copy.
In remote towns, where money was not to be
had, a dozen copies would be bought with
potatoes or wheat, and disposed of one by one,
— at the blacksmith's for a few nails; at the
tavern for rum; at some neighbor's in payment
of a trifling debt. Chapmen carried them in
their packs to exchange with copper kettles
and china bowls, for worsted stockings and
knit gloves. They were the diaries, the journals, the account books of the poor. Strung
upon a stick and hung beside the chimney-
place, they formed an unbroken record of
domestic affairs, in many instances for thirty
years. On the margins of one since picked up
at a paper mill are recorded the interesting
cases of a physician's practice, and the names
of those who suffered with the smallpox and
the flux. Another has become a complete

journal of farm life. A third is filled with verses written in imitation of Pope and Young.

It is not by mere chance that the second piece of printing done in the colonies, and the first piece done in the middle states, were almanacs. Samuel Atkins told no more than plain truth when, in the preface to " Kalendarium Pennsilvaniense," he declared that wherever he went in his travels he found the people so clamorous for an almanac that he was " really troubled," and did design according to his knowledge to "pleasure his countrymen " with what they wanted.

But one attempt at almanac-making was enough for Atkins, and the next year Daniel Leeds took his place. Leeds describes himself as a " Student in Agriculture ; " but jack-of-all-trades would have been more just. Unquestionably a man of parts, he was by turns a cooper, a surveyor-general, a member of the assembly, a member of the New Jersey provincial council, a book - maker, an almanac-maker, and, save one, the most prolific of all writers on the great schism stirred up by Keith. Even now his " News of a Trumpet," his " Trumpet Sounded," his " Hue and Cry," and his " Great Mystery of Fox-craft Discovered," are said to be far from tedious. But even Leeds, shrewd as he was, had not learned the art of almanac-making, put in what he intended for wit and fun, and brought down upon himself the anger of the Friends. The Burlington meeting condemned his almanac and bade him print nothing he had not first shown to them. The Philadelphia meeting bought up the edition, suppressed it, and not one copy is extant. Leeds in alarm humbled himself in the dust, admitted that he had sinned, promised to write more soberly in the future, soon became an Episcopalian, and thenceforth reviled and was reviled by the Friends.

When Bradford left Philadelphia, Leeds's almanac went with him to New York, and for six years no such work was printed in Pennsylvania. But with the revival of printing in 1699 a new crop of philomaths, students in agriculture, and philodespots sprang up and flourished exceedingly. In 1732 there were, in Philadelphia alone, the almanacs of Evans, of Birkett, of Godfrey, of Taylor, of Jerman, Der Teutsche Pilgrim, and of Titan Leeds so exquisitely ridiculed in the early issues of " Poor Richard."

The ingredients of all these books were the same. The title-page commonly did duty for a table of contents. The preface was devoted to describing the merits of what came after, to sneers at the critics of the last year's number,

and to the abuse of the works of rival philomaths. Following the preface was the naked
man bestriding the globe, the calendars of the
months, the days for holding courts and fairs,
a chronology that always went back to Adam,
a list of British rulers in which Cromwell never
had a place, verses destitute of feet and sense,
and a serious prognostication of events as fore-
told by eclipses and the planets.

In writing their almanacs, American " philomaths " without exception borrowed most freely
from English contemporaries, and from this
time-honored usage Franklin did not depart.
Richard Saunders, who long edited the " Apollo
Angelicanus," furnished the name under which
he wrote. Poor Robin supplied the hint for the
title, and many ideas for the general plan.

" Poor Robin " was an English comic almanac defaced with the indecency and licentious-
ness it was then the fashion to associate with
wit, with humor, and with broad fun. One
number is declared to be " calculated to the
meridian of all honest merry hearts ; and writ
in their language ; and fitted to all latitudes in
the temperate zone, where people are neither
hot with passion nor cold with envy, and where
the Pole is elevated ninety degrees above scandal and detraction." Another is suited " to all
latitudes and capacities whatsoever, but more

especially those that have got sixpence to spare to buy an almanac." A third bears the title, " Poor Robin. A prognostication for the year of our Lord God 1725, wherein you have a scheme (not for a Lottery, nor the South Sea) but for the use of Astrologers, with an account of the eclipses, and a great many more than any other almanac mentions, with predictions about courtings, weddings, &c., the like not extant."

The account of the eclipses which no other almanac mentions might have been written by Poor Richard himself. Indeed it is closely paralleled in his prognostication for 1739.

With a few hints borrowed from these two sources, Franklin began the publication of " Poor Richard " in October, 1732. The success was immense. Before the month ended the first impression was exhausted. When the year closed, the third edition was offered for sale. Not a little of this popularity is, we believe, to be ascribed to the air of reality that pervades the whole book. To those who read " Poor Robin " then, as to those who read him now, he was a mere name, a mask to hide another name. Poor Richard was a person, almost as real to those who read him as King George or Governor Penn, or any of the famous men of whom they were constantly hearing but never meeting face to face. It is high praise, but not too high praise, to say, that Mr. Richard Saunders and Bridget his wife are quite as real as any characters in the whole domain of fiction.

Indeed the prefaces to the almanacs in which they appear form, collectively, a piece of prose fiction which for humor, for sprightliness, for the knowledge of human nature displayed, is well worthy of perusal. In the first of the prefaces Mr. Saunders set forth the reasons for adding one more to the long list of almanac-makers. He might, he declares, assert the sole aim he had in view was the public good. But men are not to be deceived by such pretenses, and the plain truth is, he is excessive poor, while his wife, poor woman, is excessive proud. She could no longer bear to sit spinning in her shift of tow, while he did nothing but gaze at the stars. More than once had she threatened to burn his books and rattling-traps if he did not make some use of them for the good of his family. At last he had complied with his dame's desire and given to the world an almanac, a thing he would have done long before had he not been fearful of doing harm to his old friend and fellow-student Titan Leeds. But this fear troubled him no longer, for Titan was soon to be numbered with the immortals.

Death, never known to respect merit, had already prepared the mortal dart; the fatal sister had already extended her destroying shears, and that ingenious man must surely perish on October 17, 1733, at the very moment of the ☌ of ☉ and ☿. Since, therefore, the provinces were to see no more of Leeds's performances, he felt free to take up the task.

Twenty-seven years before, Jacob Taylor, a rival philomath, described the father of Titan as " that unparalleled Plagiary and unreasonable transcriber, D. Leeds, who hath, with a very large stock of impudence, filched matter out of another man's works to furnish his spurious almanacs." The description is applicable to the whole race of philomaths, but applies with especial force to the Leeds, father and sons. But Titan was the fool positive, and as fair a butt for wit as the province produced. What a jest was he never knew. So he took the pleasantry of Poor Richard for sober earnest, and replied. He denounced Poor Richard as an ignorant and presumptuous predicter, called him a liar, a fool, a conceited scribbler, and declared that, by God's blessing, Titan Leeds should live and write long after Poor Richard Saunders and his almanac were dead and forgotten.

This reply was precisely what Franklin expected, and in the preface to Poor Richard for 1734 the public is assured that, thanks to its bounty, " Poor Dick " is far from dying. Now Bridget not only had a pot of her own, with something to put in it, but two new shifts, a pair of shoes and a new warm petticoat, while Richard, dressed in a good second-hand coat, was no longer ashamed to show himself in town. As for Titan Leeds, he did die at the very hour and minute predicted. This was evident because of the harsh language of his pretended preface, for Mr. Leeds was too civil a man to use an old friend so shamefully: because the stars had predicted his death and they were not to be disappointed; because it was necessary that he should die punctually at the hour named for the honor of astrology, an art professed by him and by his father before him; and because the almanacs were too bad to be the work of Titan Leeds if living. The wit was low and flat. The little hints were dull. There was nothing smart in the almanac but Hudibras verses against astrology, which no astrologer but a dead one would ever have inserted. As for the rest, no man living could or would have written such stuff. Again Leeds took the fun in earnest and replied. " Poor Richard " had used him with such good manners that he hardly knew what to say. But this he would say of Mr. Saunders's boasted

prosperity : " If Falsehood and Ingenuity be so
rewarded, what may he expect if he be in a
capacity to publish what is either just or according to Art."

Thus dismissed, Leeds disappears from the
almanacs for five years, and the prefaces are
taken up with other matters. One is given to
insisting that "Poor Richard " does exist, for
the public have begun to suspect that he is
none other than Franklin. Another is a defense of almanac-makers. That some of their
predictions failed was not amazing. Without
any defect in the art itself, it was easy to see
that a small error, a single wrong figure over-
seen in a long calculation, might cause great
mistakes. But, however almanac-makers might
miss it in other things, it must be allowed they
always hit the day of the month, and that after
all was one of the most useful things in an
almanac. As to the weather, he never followed
the method of his brother John Jerman. Jerman would say, " Snow here or in New England," " Rain here or in South Carolina,"
" Cold to the Northward," " Warm to the
Southward." This enabled him to hide his
errors. For if it did not rain here, who could
say it did not rain in New England. Poor
Richard always put down just what the weather
will be where the reader is, only asking for an

allowance of a day or two before and a day or two after. If the prediction failed then, why like enough the printer had transferred or misplaced it to make room for his holidays. As the public would give Mr. Printer credit for making the almanacs, let him also take some of the blame.

A third explains how astrologers determine what the weather will be, and is just witty enough and coarse enough to have been thought good reading.

A fourth was from the hand of Bridget Saunders. Her good man had set out for the Potomac to meet an old Stargazer. Before going he left a copy of his almanac sealed up and bade her send it to the printer. Suspecting something was wrong, she opened it to see if he had not been flinging some of his old skits at her. So it was. Peascods! could she not have a little fault but the world must be told of it? They had already been told that she was proud; that she was poor; that she had a new petticoat, and abundance more of the like stuff. Now they must know she had taken a fancy to drink a little tea. She had cut this nonsense out. Looking over the months, she found a great quantity of foul weather. She had cut this out also, and put in fine weather for housewives to dry their clothes in.

Yet another preface is written by the ghost of his old friend Titan Leeds.

Leeds by this time was really dead, and that the world might know the letter to be the work of his ghost, the ghost made three predictions for the coming year. A certain well-known character would remain sober for nine consecutive hours, to the great astonishment of his friends; William and Andrew Bradford would put out another "Leeds' Almanac" just as if Leeds were still alive; and that John Jerman on the 17th of September would become reconciled to the Church of Rome. On the fulfilment of these predictions rested the truth of the ghost.

Jerman for twenty years past had been the author of a Quaker almanac, and had for about the same time been engaged in a fierce almanac warfare with Jacob Taylor, a philomath and a printer of Friends' books. Jerman seems to have been as thick-headed as Leeds, took the same course as Leeds, repelled the charge, and the next year boasted that he had not gone over to Rome, and denounced Poor Richard as one of the false prophets of Baal. He could have done nothing more to Poor Richard's mind; and in the preface to "Poor Richard" for 1742 the whole town read with delight the evidence of Jerman's conversion, which, despite

his declaring and protesting, " is, I fear," said
Mr. Saunders, " too true." Two things in the
elegiac verses confirmed this suspicion. The
1st of November was called All-Hallows Day.
Did not this smell of Popery? Did it in the
least savor of the plain language of Friends?
But the plainest evidence of all was the adora-
tion of saints which Jerman confessed to be his
practice in the lines —

> " When any trouble did me befall
> To my dear Mary then I would call."

" Did he think the whole world was so stupid
as not to notice this? So ignorant as not to
know that all Catholics paid the highest regard
to the Virgin Mary? Ah, friend John, we must
allow you to be a poet, but you certainly are
no Protestant. I could heartily wish your religion were as good as your verses."

With this the humorous prefaces cease, and
their place is taken by short pieces, which, as
Poor Richard said, were likely to do more good
than three hundred and seventy-five prefaces
written by himself. These pieces were commonly borrowed from standard works, and contain hints for growing timber, for fencing, and
accounts of how people live on the shores of
Hudson Bay and under the Tropic of Cancer.

The humor of the almanacs is by no means
confined to the prefaces. The books abound

in wit and in wit noticeable for its modern character. Now it appears in some doggerel verses at the heads of the pages ; now in the turn given to a maxim, as, " Never take a wife till you have a house (and a fire) to put her in ; " now in some pretended prognostication, as that for August, 1739, " Ships sailing down the Delaware Bay this month shall hear at ten leagues' distance a confused rattling noise like a swarm of hail on a cake of ice. Don't be frightened, good passengers, the sailors can inform you that 't is nothing but Lower County teeth in the ague. In a southerly wind you may hear it at Philadelphia."

In 1748 the size of the almanac was much enlarged, and the name changed to " Poor Richard Improved." After 1748 it is quite likely " Poor Richard " was no longer written by Franklin. While still in his hands, Franklin contributed to its pages some of the brief pieces by which he is best known. Scattered among profitable observations, eclipses, and monthly calendars are to be found his " Hints for those that would be Rich," his " Rules of Health," his " Plan for saving one hundred thousand pounds to New Jersey," and his masterpiece, "Father Abraham's Address."

In the first number of " Poor Richard," Franklin adopted the custom, long common

among "philomaths," of filling the spaces between the remarkable days in the monthly calendars with maxims of thrift, saws, and pithy
sayings, the purpose of which has been stated
by Franklin himself. " Observing that it
["Poor Richard "] was generally read, scarce
any neighborhood in the province being without it, I considered it as a proper vehicle for
conveying instruction among the common people who bought scarcely any other book. I
therefore filled all the little spaces that oc-
curred between the remarkable days in the cal-
endar with proverbial sentences, chiefly such as
inculcated industry and frugality, as the means
of procuring wealth and thereby securing virtue ; it being more difficult for a man in want
to act always honestly, as, to use here one of
those proverbs, ' It is hard for an empty sack
to stand upright.' "

But the difference between such sayings as
set forth by Poor Richard, and such sayings as
set forth by Jerman or Leeds, is often just the
difference between sense and nonsense, meaning
and gibberish. It is hardly possible to read a
page of Leeds without being told that " There 's
knavery in the wind ; " that " The cat ate the
candle ; " that " Cully, Mully, Puff appears ; "
and that " The World is bad with somebody."
Of this sort of folly Mr. Saunders was never

guilty. And even when Leeds did drop into sense and meaning, what he says can always be found better said by Poor Richard. "Necessity," says Leeds, "is a mighty weapon." "Necessity," says Poor Richard, "never made a good bargain." "Be careful of the main chance," says Leeds, "or it will never take care of you;" "Keep thy shop," says Poor Dick, "and thy shop will keep thee." "'T is best," says Leeds, "to make a good use of another's folly." "Fools," says Poor Richard, "make feasts, and wise men eat them." "Bad hours and ill company have ruined many fine young people," says Leeds. Put into the language of Poor Richard this becomes, "The rotten apple spoils his companion."

For wisdom of this kind Franklin claimed neither reading nor invention. Much he took bodily from Poor Robin and Gadbury, who in turn took them from Ray.[1] Much more he

---

[1] Ray's book, called *A Collection of English Proverbs*, was printed at Cambridge, 1678. A few proverbs will serve as examples.

RAY.

God healeth and the physician hath the thanks.

Marry your sons when you will; your daughters when you can.

God sends meat and the devil cooks.

POOR RICHARD.

God heals and the doctor takes the fee.

Marry your sons when you will; but your daughters when you can.

Bad commentation spoils the best of books:

So God sends meat (they say) the devil cooks.

borrowed from humbler writers and dressed in his own words. But wherever it came from, there can be no doubt that it had much to do with the immense popularity of the almanac. Mr. Saunders became a personage as well known in that age as Josh Billings and Mrs. Partington in ours. He became a type, and more than one piece of wisdom he never was guilty of writing owed its currency to the words " As Poor Richard says." His sayings passed into the daily speech of the people, were quoted in sermons, were printed on the title-pages of pamphlets and used as mottoes by the newspaper moralists of the day, and continued down even to the Revolution to be read with avidity. Then, in an hour of great need, a copy of one of the almanacs fell into the hands of Paul Jones of glorious memory. The story is told, that, after his famous victory in " The Ranger," he went to Brest to await the coming of the new ship so often promised him ; that month after month he was tormented by excuses and delays ; that he wrote to Franklin, to the royal family, to the King, begging that a vessel might be given him ; that, wellnigh distracted, he happened to pick up a copy of " Poor Richard," and read, " If you would have

See a note by Dr. S. A. Green, in *Hist. Magazine*, Jan'y, 1860, pp. 16, 17.

your business done, go; if not, send;" that he
took the hint, hurried to Versailles, and there
got an order for the purchase of the ship which
he renamed, in honor of his teacher, "Bon
Homme Richard."

Nothing, perhaps, shows the fondness of the
people for the sayings of Mr. Saunders better
than the history of that famous piece in which
the best of them are brought together. It
came out in a day of darkness and of gloom.
The French and Indian war had been raging
for four years; and success was still with the
French. Washington had been driven from
Fort Necessity. Braddock had perished in the
woods. The venture against Niagara had failed.
That against Ticonderoga had done little.
The sea swarmed with French and Spanish
privateers. Trade was dull. Taxes were heavy.
Grumbling was everywhere. Men of all sorts
bemoaned the hard times. The war ought to
stop. The assemblies, the grumblers said, ought
to put out more credit bills. The mother country ought to pay the cost of colonial troops.
Were every one of these remedies used they
could not, Franklin thought, cure the hard
times. Economy and thrift alone could do so.
Here then was a fine chance for a sermon by
"Poor Richard" with a reasonable hope of being heard. A sermon was accordingly written,

put in the mouth of a wise old man called Father Abraham, and published in the almanac for 1758. It was pretended that "Poor Richard" had heard the speech at an auction. A fitter place Father Abraham could not have chosen; for the auctions of those days were shameful scenes of extravagance and folly. Called thither by bell and crier, the people gathered long before the hour named, were plied with rum at the cost of the vendue master till, when the sale opened, they offered bids and paid prices such as never would have been had from them in their sober senses. To a throng of this sort Father Abraham spoke. What he said, with a few words by "Poor Richard," is as follows: —

I have heard, that nothing gives an author so great pleasure as to find his works respectfully quoted by other learned authors. This pleasure I have seldom enjoyed; for, though I have been, if I may say it without vanity, an eminent author (of almanacs) annually, now, a full quarter of a century, my brother authors in the same way, for what reason I know not, have ever been very sparing in their applauses; and no other author has taken the least notice of me; so that, did not my writings produce me some solid pudding, the great deficiency of praise would have quite discouraged me. I concluded, at length, that the people were the best judges of my merit for they buy my works ; and besides, in my rambles, where I am not personally known, I have frequently heard one or other of my adages repeated, with "As Poor Richard says," at the end on 't. This gave me some satisfaction, as it showed not only that my instructions were regarded, but discovered likewise some respect for my authority ; and I own, that, to encourage the practice of remembering and reading those wise sentences, I have sometimes quoted myself with great gravity. Judge, then, how much I must have been gratified by an incident I am going to relate to you. I stopped my horse lately, where a great number of people were collected at an auction of merchants' goods. The hour of the sale not being come, they were conversing on the badness of the times ; and one of the company called to a plain, clean, old man, with white locks, " Pray, Father Abraham, what think you of the times ? will not these heavy taxes quite ruin the country ; how shall we ever be able to pay them ? What would you advise us to do ? " Father Abraham stood up, and replied, " If you would have my advice, I will give it to you in short ; for, A word to the wise is enough, as Poor Richard says." They joined in desiring him to speak his mind, and gathering around him, he proceeded as follows : —

"Friends," said he, " the taxes are indeed very heavy, and, if those laid on by the government were the only ones we had to pay, we might more easily discharge them ; but we have many others, and much more grievous to some of us. We are taxed twice as much by our idleness, three times as much by our pride, and four times as much by our folly ; and from these taxes the commissioners can not ease or deliver us, by allowing an abatement. However, let us hearken to good advice, and something may be done for us ; God helps them that help themselves, as Poor Richard says.

"I. It would be thought a hard government that should task its people one tenth part of their time, to be employed in its service ; but idleness taxes many of us much more ; sloth, by bringing on diseases, absolutely shortens life. Sloth, like rust, consumes faster than labor wears ; while the used key is always bright, as Poor Richard says. But dost thou love life, then do not squander time, for that is the stuff life is made of, as Poor Richard says. How much more than is necessary do we spend in sleep, forgetting that The sleeping fox catches no poultry, and that There will be sleeping enough in the grave, as Poor Richard says.

" If time be of all things the most precious, wasting time must be, as Poor Richard says, the greatest prodigality ; since, as he elsewhere tells us, Lost time is never found again ; and what we call time enough always proves little enough. Let us then be up and be doing, and doing to the purpose ; so by diligence shall we do more with less perplexity. Sloth makes all things difficult, but industry, all easy ; and He that riseth late must trot all day, and shall scarce overtake his business at night ; while Laziness travels so slowly that Poverty soon overtakes him. Drive thy business, let not that drive thee; and Early to bed, and early to rise, makes a man healthy, wealthy, and wise, as Poor Richard says.

" So what signifies wishing and hoping for better times? We make these times better, if we bestir ourselves. Industry need not wish, and he that lives upon hopes will die fasting. There are no gains without pains; then help, hands, for I have no lands; or, if I have, they are smartly taxed. He that hath a trade, hath an estate; and he that hath a calling, hath an office of profit and honor, as Poor Richard says; but then the trade must be worked at, and the calling followed, or neither the estate nor the office will enable us to pay our taxes. If we are industrious, we shall never starve; for, At the workingman's house hunger looks in, but dares not enter. Nor will the bailiff or the constable enter; for, Industry pays debts, while despair increaseth them. What though you have found no treasure, nor has any rich relation left you a legacy; Diligence is the mother of good luck, and God gives all things to Industry. Then plow deep while sluggards sleep, and you shall have corn to sell and to keep. Work while it is called to-day, for you know not how much you may be hindered to-morrow. One to-day is worth two to-morrows, as Poor Richard says; and further, Never leave that till to-morrow which you can do to-day. If you were a servant, would you not be ashamed that a good master should catch you idle? Are you then your own master? Be ashamed to catch your-self idle, when there is so much to be done for your-

self, your family, your country, your king. Handle
your tools without mittens; remember that The cat in
gloves catches no mice, as Poor Richard says. It is
true there is much to be done, and perhaps you are
weak-handed; but stick to it steadily, and you will
see great effects; for, Constant dropping wears away
stones; and By diligence and patience the mouse
ate in two the cable; and Little strokes fell great
oaks.

"Methinks I hear some of you say, Must a man
afford himself no leisure? I will tell thee, my friend,
what Poor Richard says: Employ thy time well, if
thou meanest to gain leisure; and since thou art not
sure of a minute, throw not away an hour. Leisure is
time for doing something useful; this leisure the diligent man will obtain, but the lazy man never; for, A
life of leisure and a life of laziness are two things.
Many, without labor, would live by their wits only,
but they break for want of stock; whereas, industry
gives comfort, and plenty, and respect. Fly pleas-
ures and they will follow you. The diligent spinner
has a large shift; and now I have a sheep and a cow,
every one bids me good-morrow.

"II. But with our industry we must likewise be
steady and careful, and oversee our own affairs with
our own eyes, and not trust too much to others; for,
as poor Richard says, —

> I never saw an oft-removed tree,
> Nor yet an oft-removed family,
> That throve so well as those that settled be.

And again, Three removes are as bad as a fire; and

again, Keep thy shop, and thy shop will keep thee; and again, If you would have your business done, go; if not, send. And again, —

> He that by the plough would thrive,
> Himself must either hold or drive.

And again, The eye of the master will do more work than both his hands; and again, Want of care does us more damage than want of knowledge; and again, Not to oversee workmen, is to leave them your purse open. Trusting too much to others' care is the ruin of many; for, In the affairs of this world men are saved, not by faith but by the want of it; but a man's own care is profitable; for, If you would have a faithful servant, and one that you like, serve yourself. A little neglect may breed great mischief; for want of a nail the shoe was lost; for want of a shoe the horse was lost; and for want of a horse the rider was lost, being overtaken and slain by the enemy; all for want of a little care about a horseshoe nail.

" III. So much for industry, my friends, and attention to one's own business; but to these we must add frugality, if we would make our industry more certainly successful. A man may, if he knows not how to save as he gets, keep his nose all his life to the grindstone, and die not worth a groat at last. A fat kitchen makes a lean will; and —

> Many estates are spent in the getting,
> Since women forsook spinning and knitting,
> And men for punch forsook hewing and splitting.

If you would be wealthy, think of saving as well as

of getting. The Indies have not made Spain rich, because her outgoes are greater than her incomes.

" Away then with your expensive follies, and you will not then have so much cause to complain of hard times, heavy taxes, and chargeable families ; for —

> Women and wine, game and deceit,
> Make the wealth small and the want great.

And further, What maintains one vice would bring up two children. You may think, perhaps, that a little tea or a little punch now and then, diet a little more costly, clothes a little finer, and a little entertainment now and then, can be no great matter ; but remember, Many a little makes a mickle. Beware of little expenses; A small leak will sink a great ship, as Poor Richard says ; and again, Who dainties love shall beggars prove ; and moreover, Fools make feasts and wise men eat them.

" Here you are all got together at this sale of fineries and knick-knacks. You call them goods ; but, if you do not take care, they will prove evils to some of you. You expect they will be sold cheap, and perhaps they may for less than they cost ; but, if you have no occasion for them, they must be dear to you. Remember what Poor Richard says : Buy what thou hast no need of, and ere long thou shalt sell thy necessaries. And again, At a great pennyworth pause a while. He means, that perhaps the cheapness is apparent only, and not real ; or, the bargain, by straitening thee in thy business, may do thee more harm than good. For in another place he says, Many have been ruined by buying good pennyworths.

Again, It is foolish to lay out money in a purchase of repentance; and yet, this folly is practised every day at auctions, for want of minding the Almanac. Many a one, for the sake of finery on the back, have gone with a hungry belly and half-starved their families. Silks and satins, scarlet and velvets, put out the kitchen fire, as Poor Richard says.

"These are not the necessaries of life; they can scarcely be called the conveniences; and yet, only because they look pretty, how many want to have them. By these, and other extravagances, the genteel are reduced to poverty, and forced to borrow of those whom they formerly despised, but who, through industry and frugality, have maintained their standing; in which case it appears plainly, that A plowman on his legs is higher than a gentleman on his knees, as Poor Richard says. Perhaps they have a small estate left them which they knew not the getting of; they think, It is day and it never will be night: that a little to be spent out of so much is not worth minding; but Always taking out of the meal-tub, and never putting in, soon comes to the bottom, as Poor Richard says; and then, When the well is dry, they know the worth of water. But this they might have known before, if they had taken his advice. If you would know the value of money, go and try to borrow some; for He that goes a-borrowing goes a-sorrowing, as Poor Richard says; and, indeed, so does he that lends to such people, when he goes to get it in again. Poor Dick further advises, and says, —

> Fond pride of dress is sure a very curse;
> Ere fancy you consult, consult your purse.

And again, Pride is as loud a beggar as Want, and a great deal more saucy. When you have bought one fine thing, you must buy ten more, that your appearance may be all of a piece; but Poor Dick says, It is easier to suppress the first desire, than to satisfy all that follow it. And it is as truly folly for the poor to ape the rich, as for the frog to swell in order to equal the ox.

> Vessels large may venture more,
> But little boats should keep near shore.

It is, however, a folly soon punished; for, as Poor Richard says, Pride that dines on vanity, sups on contempt. Pride breakfasted with Plenty, dined with Poverty, and supped with Infamy. And, after all, of what use is this pride of appearance, for which so much is risked, so much is suffered? It cannot promote health, nor ease pain; it makes no increase of merit in the person; it creates envy; it hastens misfortune.

"But what madness must it be to run in debt for these superfluities? We are offered by the terms of this sale, six months credit; and that, perhaps, has induced some of us to attend it, because we cannot spare the ready money, and hope now to be fine without it. But, ah! think what you do when you run in debt; you give to another power over your liberty. If you cannot pay at the time, you will be ashamed to see your creditor; you will be in fear when you speak to him; you will make poor, pitiful, sneaking excuses, and, by degrees, come to lose your veracity, and sink into base, downright lying; for The second vice is lying, the first is running in debt, as Poor Richard says; and again, to the same purpose, Lying rides upon Debt's back; whereas, a free-born Englishman ought not to be ashamed nor afraid to see or speak to any man living. But poverty often deprives a man of all spirit and virtue. It is hard for an empty bag to stand upright.

" What would you think of that prince, or of that government, who should issue an edict forbidding you to dress like a gentleman or gentlewoman, on pain of imprisonment or servitude? Would you not say that you were free, have a right to dress as you please, and that such an edict would be a breach of your privileges, and such a government tyrannical? And yet you are about to put yourself under such tyranny, when you run in debt for such dress. Your creditor has authority, at his pleasure, to deprive you of your liberty, by confining you in gaol till you shall be able to pay him. When you have got your bargain, you may, perhaps, think little of payment; but, as Poor Richard says, creditors have better memories than debtors; creditors are a superstitious sect, great observers of set days and times. The day comes round before you are aware, and the demand is made before you are prepared to satisfy it; or, if you bear your debt in mind, the term, which at first seemed so long, will, as it lessens, appear extremely short. Time will seem to have added wings to his heels as well as his shoulders. Those have a short Lent, who owe money to be paid at Easter. At present, perhaps, you may think yourselves in thriving circumstances, and that you can bear a little extravagance without injury; but —

> For age and want save while you may;
> No morning sun lasts a whole day.

Gain may be temporary and uncertain, but ever, while you live, expense is constant and certain; and It is easier to build two chimneys, than to keep one in fuel, as Poor Richard says; so, Rather go to bed supperless, than rise in debt.

> Get what you can, and what you get hold;
> 'T is the stone that will turn all your lead into gold.

And when you have got the Philosopher's stone, sure you will no longer complain of bad times, or the difficulty of paying taxes.

"IV. This doctrine, my friends, is reason and wisdom; but, after all, do not depend too much upon your own industry, and frugality, and prudence, though excellent things; for they may all be blasted, without the blessing of Heaven; and, therefore, ask that blessing humbly, and be not uncharitable to those that at present seem to want it, but comfort and help them. Remember, Job suffered, and was afterwards prosperous.

"And now, to conclude, Experience keeps a dear school, but fools will learn in no other, as Poor Richard says, and scarce in that; for, it is true, we may give advice, but we cannot give conduct. However, remember this : They that will not be counselled cannot be helped ; and further, that, If you will not hear Reason, she will surely rap your knuckles, as Poor Richard says."

Thus the old gentleman ended his harangue. The people heard it, and approved the doctrine, and immediately practised the contrary, just as if it had been a common sermon ; for the auction opened, and they began to buy extravagantly. I found the good man had thoroughly studied my almanacs, and digested all I had dropped on these topics during the course of twenty-five years. The frequent mention he made of me must have tired any one else; but my vanity was wonderfully delighted with it, though I was conscious that not a tenth part of the wisdom was my own which he ascribed to me, but rather the gleanings that I had made of the sense of all ages and nations. However, I resolved to be the better for the echo of it ; and, though I had at first determined to buy stuff for a new coat, I went away resolved to wear my old one a little longer. Reader, if thou wilt do the same, thy profit will be as great as mine. I am, as ever, thine to serve thee,

RICHARD SAUNDERS.

The praise bestowed on Father Abraham, by those who heard him at the auction stand, was soon taken up by the civilized world. The sale of the almanac had always been large. Year after year ten thousand copies, or one for every hundred inhabitants of the land, came from the press. But ten thousand copies did not begin to meet the demand for "Poor Richard" of 1758. Such was the eagerness of the people to read the Address that the newspapers published it again and again. Franklin himself sent it forth as a broadside, and at last, in 1760, his nephew, Benjamin Mecom of Boston, made it into a pamphlet, adorned with a huge folding plate of Father Abraham in his study. The title is, "Father Abraham's Speech to a great number of people, at a Vendue of Merchants' Goods; introduced to the public by Poor Richard (a famous Pennsylvanian conjurer and almanac-maker), in answer to the following questions: 'Pray, Father Abraham, what do you think of the times? Won't these heavy taxes quite ruin the country? How shall we be ever able to pay them? What would you advise us to?'"

In the Advertisement, without which no book was then thought complete, the reader is assured that "at the first appearance of this humorous and instructive production, several gentlemen of approved taste were struck with the design and beauty of it, and therefore desired to know the parents' name. Father Abraham's speech is the comely offspring of that Frank-lyn-cean genius who is the author of a pamphlet intitled 'The Interest of Great Britain Considered,'" a pamphlet Franklin did not write. Thus started by Mecom, the speech was quickly republished in the same form at New Haven, at New London, at Philadelphia.

Franklin was then at London, and thither his work followed him; was printed on a broadside, was widely circulated, was hung up on the walls of workshops and houses; crossed the Channel; was done into French, and bought in great quantity by priests and nobles for distribution among the poor. Since that day it has spread over the whole of Europe, and may now be read in French, in German, in Spanish, in Italian, in Russian, in the language of Holland, in the language of Bohemia, in modern Greek, in Gaelic, and in Portuguese. Under the title " La Science du Bonhomme Richard," it has been thirty times printed in French, and twice in Italian. As " The Way to Wealth," it has been issued twenty-seven times in English in pamphlet form, and innumerable times as a broadside. Never since 1770 has a period of five years been suffered to go by without a new edition of " The Way to Wealth " appearing in some form in some language. Printers have used it to advertise their business. Short-hand writers have issued it in phonetic characters. It may be found in the publications of societies for improving the condition of the poor; in " Prompters;" in " Immortal Men-

tors ; " in " Moral Tracts ; " in " First Notions
of Political Economy ; " in " Elements of Morals ; " in " Whole Duties of Men and Women,"
and as a rebus for the amusement of the idle.
Without question, the speech of Father Abraham is the most famous piece of literature the
colonies produced. After 1758 Franklin wrote
no more for " Poor Richard." In 1796 the
almanac ceased to appear.

In 1740 Franklin embarked in a literary
venture of which no mention is made in the
Autobiography. That he should remember so
much that was passing and trivial, and forget
this, is strange indeed. The newspaper quarrel with which it opened, and the flat failure
in which it closed, might well have served to
keep it in mind. But it did not.

The venture was a magazine. No such publication had then appeared in the English
colonies ; but the time for one was now come,
he thought, and, thinking so, he began to look
about him for some one to act as editor. The
person chosen was John Webbe, a conveyancer
and a dull pedant, now remembered by gather-
ers of rare old books as the author of a pamphlet entitled " A Discourse Concerning Paper
Money." To him the plan was fully unfolded,
the terms of publication settled, and a bargain
made, when, in the " Mercury " of October

30, 1740, Webbe announced a magazine of
his own. His prospectus filled just one half
of the newspaper, and would in our times be
enough to kill a magazine outright. The encouragement given to magazines in England
was his excuse for attempting one in America.
But he would by no means follow the British
models. He had a plan of his own, and his
plan was this: In his magazine should be
found speeches of governors; addresses of assemblies; extracts of laws, with the reasons on
which they were founded and the ills they were
to remove; accounts of the climate, soil, productions, trades and manufactures of the British
colonies; of trials, of the course of exchange,
of the fluctuation of paper money; but no
scandal, no falsehood, no defamatory libeling.
Then followed a long, dreary, and pedantic
essay on the horridness of defamation, on the
law of libel, on the liberty of the press, and
the duty of obedience to rulers, mingled with
scraps from Euripides and Horace. In a
"postscript" he announced that the magazine
should issue monthly, should contain four
sheets, should cost twelve shillings Pennsylvania money a year, and should be printed by
Andrew Bradford.

In the next issue of the "Gazette" was
Franklin's plan for a magazine. The name

was to be " The General Magazine and Historical Chronicle for all the British Plantations in
America." The price to the public was to be
ninepence Pennsylvania money, but chapmen
were to have it for less. No subscriptions were
to be taken. This, he stated, had two advantages: Readers need only buy such numbers as
pleased them, while the printer would be forced
to exert himself to find such pieces as would
please them. The idea of such a magazine
had long been in his mind. Indeed, he had
chosen his writers and bought his small type.
Yet he would not have begun publication so
soon had not a person to whom he told this plan
in confidence, betrayed him, and published it in
the last " Mercury." This was to discourage
him from going on. But he would go on, and
seek, by care, by diligence, by impartiality, by
turning out a well-printed pamphlet, to have at
least a share of public favor.

Webbe now grew angry, and wrote so long
a reply that it filled all the spare columns of
three numbers of the " Mercury." He called
his reply " The Detection," and, after a great
deal of just such stuff as angry men are always
writing, began to answer the charges. Mr.
Franklin did, indeed, mention his desire to
print a magazine, and asked him to compose it.
But did such a request compel him to write one

for Mr. Franklin to print? Did it prevent him from publishing at Mr. Bradford's press without Mr. Franklin's leave? If so, then Mr. Franklin had but to offer himself as printer of books and pamphlets to every man he thought able to write them, and they would thenceforth be restrained from printing anything without his consent. As to a plan, Mr. Franklin never made a plan. Just what he did do was jotted down in his own handwriting, and was this:—

"Magazine to consist of 3 sheets, 1000 to be printed at first. Price 15s. a year, or 15d. apiece single, 12s. a Doz. to those that sell again.

"B. F. to be at all Expense of Paper, Printing, Correspondence, for procuring Materials, &c., vending, keeping accounts, &c. J. W. to dispose the Materials, make Abstracts, and write what shall be necessary for promoting the Thing, &c. The Money received to be divided thus: . . . B. F., for and towards defraying the Expense above mentioned, to take first one half, the Remainder to be equally divided between him and J. W. Bad debts, if any, to be divided in the same manner.

"To agree for a Term of 7 years. The above Agreement to be for all under 2000; all above 2000 sold, the money to be equally divided; B. F. to be at all Expense."

When these proposals were delivered to Webbe, Franklin declared that he was entitled to half the profits, beside his gain as a printer, for two reasons. In the first place, he had a font of small letter such as no other printer in America had; in the second place, he was postmaster, and that gave him power to circulate his magazine to the exclusion of any rival. Believing all this, Webbe readily agreed. But before the contract was engrossed and ready for signing, he grew wiser. The reasons for claiming so great a share of the profits he learned were groundless and ridiculous, and, fearing grosser frauds behind, he carried his plan to Bradford. If Bradford gave him better terms, it was not because he loved Webbe, but because he hated Franklin.

The second installment of "The Detection" is given to sneering at Franklin's plan, to justifying Webbe's plan, but at the same time assuring the public that the proposed magazine will not appear. In the third number of "The Detection," Webbe flatly accused Franklin of using his place of postmaster to shut the "Mercury" out of the post, and of refusing to let the riders carry it with the "Gazette." Up to this point in the squabble Franklin had made no reply. He now dropped the advertisement of the magazine, and in its place put a letter.

It was true that none of Bradford's "Mercuries" were carried by the riders. Colonel Spotswood, the postmaster-general, had peremptorily forbidden it; and he had forbidden it because Mr. Bradford had persistently refused to settle his accounts as late postmaster at Philadelphia.

The dispute had now become so hot that Bradford issued a postscript to the "Mercury," in which Webbe made a rambling reply. It was true that, after the orders of Colonel Spotswood, no more "Mercuries" had been sent to the post-office to be forwarded in the mail; but they had been sent to the riders, and had, with the connivance of Franklin, been distributed by them. Now, upon a sudden, this was stopped, and it was stopped because of the letters which the "Mercury" contained. This charge undoubtedly was true.

With this the quarrel ended, and no more was heard of the magazines till the close of January, 1740–1741. Then, to the surprise of the town, Bradford announced that he had in press and would soon publish "The American Magazine, or A Monthly View of the Political State of the British Colonies." True to his word, the magazine was on his counter on the 13th of February, 1740–1741. Three days later Franklin issued "The General Magazine and

Historical Chronicle for all the British Provinces in America." "The American Magazine" lived three months, and was ridiculed
by Franklin in doggerel verse. "The General
Magazine" struggled on for six months, and
then quietly expired. It was printed on the
small type of which Franklin had boasted to
Webbe. The title-page was adorned with the
Prince of Wales' coronet and plumes. The
contents were historical, political, religious.
There were speeches of governors, replies of
assemblies, pieces of poetry, extracts from
books, long theological disputes, and a man-
ual of arms. But neither the contents, nor the
fine type, nor the place of postmaster, could
make it popular. It perished miserably, was
utterly forgotten by its founder, and is of no
interest now save that, with the "American
Magazine" of Bradford, it forms the first
attempt to set up the monthly magazine in
America.

CHAPTER V.

1743–1756.

THE failure of the magazine did not dishearten him, and he was soon casting about for something else to set agoing. He found it in the " Academy and Charitable School of the Province of Pennsylvania." There was in almost every large town in the province a school of some sort where the rudiments of education were taught. But nowhere did an academy, or anything approaching to a college, exist. That none existed was, to Franklin, a good and sufficient reason why he should seek to found one. It was not long, therefore, before he had a plan drawn and a rector chosen. The rector was to be the Reverend Richard Peters. But Mr. Peters had a better-paying place in view, would not think of such a position ; and Franklin, knowing of no other fit for the trust, laid his scheme aside for six years.

Hard upon the abandonment of the plan for an academy came his " Proposal for Promoting Useful Knowledge among the British Plantations in America." The paper is dated May 14, 1743, goes over the difficulties scientific men found in communicating their discoveries to each other, and suggests as a remedy the founding of the "American Philosophical Society" at Philadelphia. This was done. But beyond this fact and the roll of membership, nothing concerning it is known. The records are gone. The transactions are lost, and if any papers were communicated by the members, they too are wanting. Franklin did, indeed, propose to publish an American Philosophical Miscellany, to issue the first number in January, 1746, and to put in it selections from the papers written by the gentlemen of the society. But when 1746 came Franklin was deep in electrical researches, from which in 1747 he was suddenly turned aside by a series of events it is now necessary to narrate.

In 1739 trouble broke out between England and Spain as to the right to gather salt at Tortugas and cut logwood at Campeachy. As the next ship from London might bring news of open war, the governor begged the assembly to put the province in a state of defense. He reminded them in strong terms of the terrors of war, of sacked cities, of ravaged fields, of the slaughter of the young and feeble by merciless and pitiless invaders. But his eloquence could not move them and they adjourned. On re-assembling, the governor again appealed for money with which to make ready for war. But he was reminded by the assembly that in Pennsylvania all men enjoyed an equal right to the liberty of conscience; that the Quakers could not in conscience take up arms, and that to compel them so to do would be a violation of the fundamental doctrines of the constitution. To exempt the Quakers from military service would, on the other hand, be to make a partial law, and to make partial laws was unconstitutional and impolitic. In short, he was plainly told that the Quakers would neither fight themselves, nor openly furnish means for others to fight. Even when war was formally declared from the court-house steps, he could obtain nothing, and was forced to be content with drumming up volunteers for an expedition " to plunder Cuba."

The proclamation which the governor put forth on that occasion, and which Franklin printed, is a fine commentary on the warfare of that age. It reads like such a speech as might have been made to the braves who sacked Schenectady, or such an exhortation as Blackbeard might have made on the eve of battle to the wretches that constituted his pirate crew.

" The Spaniards," the humane governor announced, "have no strength either of men or fortifications that can resist the king's forces on this expedition; they will be an easy conquest and you the gainers. They will fly before you and leave their houses, their negroes, their money, plate, jewels, and plantations to be possessed by you and your posterity forever.

"Consider the terms, too, on which you are invited to this undertaking. It is not at your or your country's expense. No! the king defrays the whole charge. He pays you. He clothes you. He arms you. He transports you to the places of victory, plunder, and riches, and then transports you hither again if you choose to return. . . . Would you throw off your homespun, and shine in silver and gold lace and embroidery? Would you grow rich at once? Would you leave great estates to your posterity? Go volunteer in this expedition and take the island of Cuba."

So alluring did the prospect seem, that seven companies were soon enlisted and quartered in the towns near Philadelphia; and of these troops fully three hundred were redemptioners who had volunteered for the king's service without their masters' consent. Out of this grew a long dispute between the governor and the assembly, which neither the appearance of Spanish privateers off the coast, nor the declaration of war with France, nor the arrival of a French privateer at the Capes, nor the rejoicings which followed the capture of Louisburg, could quite compose.

When news came that the fleet had actually sailed, the desire to hear of its success became intense. "My shop," Franklin wrote to his brother John, " is filled with thirty inquirers at the coming in of every post. Some wonder the place is not yet taken. I tell them I shall be glad to hear that news three months hence." When he did hear it the city was made wild with joy. Bells were rung, bonfires lighted, toasts drunk, and whole days spent in visits of congratulation. Then at last the Quakers yielded a trifle, and placed four thousand pounds in the hands of two trustees " to purchase bread, beef, pork, flour, wheat or other grain to be used in the king's service as the governor shall think best." The story has come down to us that the governor declared " other grain " meant powder, and that for powder the money was spent.

Be this as it may, the time for such trifling was soon to end. On the morning of July 12, 1747, a sloop came to anchor just off Cape May, ran up the English colors, and signaled for a pilot to come on board. The first to see her obeyed, and clambered up her side to find himself on the deck of a French privateer commanded by French officers and manned by a Spanish crew. Seizing the pilot-boat, an officer and some men sailed into the Delaware, landed near New Castle, plundered two houses, beat a man, shot a woman, and carried off a negro wench. As they passed down the river they robbed a second pilot-boat of sails.

Even these outrages, perpetrated within twenty miles of the town, did not move the Quakers to put the province in a state of defense. The president of the city council was not in town. But the members assembled, and declared that the province and the lower counties ought to be defended. Unhappily they had no money, the assembly was not sitting, and the assembly alone could provide the money. In this strait some merchants offered to advance the sum needed if the members of the assembly would promise to support a bill to pay them back. The city members were instantly summoned: the speaker and four others attended, heard the proposition, and firmly answered No! They would as soon, they said, take a commission to fight. Nor would the assembly, when it met, do anything. There was nothing to fear. The late danger was past and gone. No future attack was to be feared: the city was too far from the sea. Three days after this stupid answer of the assembly a

French privateer sailed up the Delaware, and a second time the city was filled with alarm. Before a fortnight had passed the Spanish privateers entered the river, and the men of Lewiston were three days under arms. Even then the assembly could only lament that such things could be.

While these events were happening on the river, Franklin was deep in the study of electricity. No study, he declared in a letter written in 1747, had ever before so completely taken up his attention and his time. What with making experiments by himself, and repeating them before friends who came in crowds to see, he had, he wrote, leisure for little else. But, the moment the assembly refused to defend the city and the province, Franklin put away his Leyden jars, turned once more to public affairs, and wrote a pamphlet which he called " Plain Truth."

The date of publication was long in doubt. One biographer has placed it in 1744 ; another somewhere between 1746 and 1747. Had either of them taken the pains to examine the " Pennsylvania Gazette " for Thursday, November 12, 1747, he might there have read, " Next Saturday will be published ' Plain Truth ; or, Serious Considerations on the Present State of the City of Philadelphia and Province of Penn-

sylvania, by a Tradesman of Philadelphia.'"
Then followed a long quotation from Sallust.

Having thus announced the pamphlet, Franklin went on to advertise it in his characteristic
way, wrote a couple of pieces in praise of it and
inserted them in the "Gazette" of November
19. One was a translation of the Latin quotation, with a few lines by way of preface signed
"X" and addressed to "Mr. Franklin." The
other he pretended came from a Presbyterian.
"Whereas," it began, "in a paper called 'Plain
Truth,' lately published, there are several in-
jurious Reflections on a number of Persons, who
the Writer calls the Party opposed to the Quakers, as if they were utterly regardless of the
Public Good, and from mean and unjustifiable
motives would refuse to do any Thing for the
Defence of the Country, some of those supposed
to be pointed at think it a Justice due to themselves and others to declare, that whatever might
have been the inconsiderate Expressions of a
few, during the Heat of our late Party Differ-
ences, they always have been and now are sin
cerely and heartily determined to exert themselves, according to their several Abilities, for
our common Security. Which may the more
easily gain Belief when it is considered they
were many of them at large Expense the Summer past in defraying the charge of a vessel

sent out as a Guard-a-Coast, and that it cost some of them (being owners) Six Hundred Pounds beyond what they gave by Subscription. And tho' they think they have great Reason to resent the abuse and unjustifiable Treatment given them by that Writer, yet they waive every Thing of this kind, in consideration of his appearing to mean well. And they do hereby further declare, that if he or any other Person can propose a practicable Scheme by which the Inhabitants of this Province may be united and disciplined, and the county and city put into a state of Defence, none shall enter into the same more heartily than they."

The sole purpose for which this pretended criticism was written is set forth in the closing sentence. At the end of his pamphlet Franklin promised his readers that he would, if his hints met their approval, lay before them, in a few days, a plan of an association for defense. He now in his criticism called upon himself to furnish " a practical scheme," and speedily did so. We are told in the Autobiography that he made ready a draft, appointed a meeting of townsmen at the New Building, harangued the people, distributed pens, ink, and copies of the plan, and that, when the papers were gathered, twelve hundred men were found to have signed. This, unhappily, is not true. Franklin wrote his account forty-one years after the event described; he had then forgotten what really took place, and what really took place appears from his own newspaper to have been this : [1] —

"Last Saturday a great number of the Inhabitants of this City met at Mr. Walton's School-House in Arch Street, when a Form of an Association for our common Security and Defense against the enemy was consider'd and agreed to. On Monday following the same was laid before a great meeting of the principal Gentlemen, Merchants and others, at Roberts' Coffee House, where, after due Debate, it was unanimously approv'd of, and another meeting appointed for the next Day following at the New Building, in order to begin signing. According, on Tuesday Evening upwards of five hundred men of all Ranks subscribed their names ; and as the Subscribing is still going on briskly in all parts of the Town, 'tis not doubted but that in a few Days the number will exceed a thousand in this City, exclusive of the neighboring Towns and Country."

To enforce precept with illustration was one of Franklin's many hobbies. He accordingly made a rude cut, in type metal, of the wagoner beseeching Hercules for aid, and stamped it on the title-page of the first edition of "Plain

[1] *Pennsylvania Gazette*, November 26, 1747.

Truth." The picture was a fitting emblem of
the principles and effect of the pamphlet. No
sooner did the people begin to bestir themselves in their own behalf than help came in
from every side. The merchants addressed the
board of trade, and begged that a man-of-war
might occasionally be sent into Delaware Bay.
The mayor and common council proposed a
letter to the proprietaries asking cannon. A
lottery was started to raise three thousand
pounds to build a battery. The common council took two thousand tickets, and the fire companies were asked to take their share. Then
began one of those foolish contests with which
the history of every sect of rigid extremists
abounds. The majority of the members of each
fire company were Friends, and the Friends
were set against both lotteries and war. In
the Union, of which Franklin was a member,
the contest seems to have been short. Of the
thirty members, twenty-two were Quakers. On
the appointed night the eight who were not
Quakers met promptly in the company room,
while as many more Quakers friendly to the
lottery gathered at a neighboring tavern, to
be called in if necessary. But they were not
wanted, for only one Quaker came to oppose
the plan, and the sixty pounds of stock were
voted to the lottery by eight votes to one. Not

expecting any aid from the Quakers, Franklin had made ready a plan of his own. "If," said he to Mr. Syng, — "if we fail, let us move the purchase of a fire-engine with the money; the Quakers can have no objection to that; and then, if you nominate me and I you as a committee for that purpose, we will buy a great gun, and certainly that will be a fire-engine."

A very different scene, however, took place at the meeting of another company. One of the members was John Smith, a Quaker, and a brother of that Samuel Smith who is now remembered for his "History of New Jersey" and his pamphlet "Necessary Truth." His journal is still preserved, and under date of November 31, 1747, he asserts that he spent the evening with his fire company; that defense and the association were much the subject of conversation, and that he said little till it was proposed to use the bank stock for the purchase of tickets, and vote on the question by ballot; that he then stoutly opposed this private method of voting; declared that he believed many would vote "yes" by ballot who would vote "no" on a show of hands; reminded them that to discourage lotteries was the duty of Friends; and carried his point against using the stock by nineteen to three.

But the battery did not suffer on that account.

The carpenters gave their labor in building it; the governor of New York loaned some cannon; while the women of the city bought the drums, halberds, banners, half-pikes, and spontoons for the twenty companies of which the Philadelphia regiment was composed. Before peace was made in 1748, eighty companies were learning their drill, the Association Battery was finished, a guard regularly mounted there each night, and every householder asked to be ready to light his windows with candles if the militia should be summoned to the battery to repel a night attack.

That "Plain Truth" had much to do with this sudden rise of martial spirit is undoubted. Two editions of the pamphlet were called for in a month. It was translated into German and read by the farmers of Northumberland and Bucks. It was promptly answered in "Necessary Truth," and provoked so bitter a wrangle that, before the year went out, six pamphlets were written and three sermons preached on the lawfulness of a man defending what is his own.

There was most happily no use for the battery or the troops. The treaty of Aix-la-Chapelle brought peace to Europe, and with the return of peace Franklin went back to his schemes of reform.

He was now without doubt the most popular man in town. And while this run of popularity lasted he determined to start his long-cherished scheme of an academy. His notions of what an academy should be were hastily gathered, a pamphlet written, and the subscribers to the "Gazette" surprised, on unfolding their newspapers one day in 1749, to find the pamphlet inside. The title was, " Proposals relating to the education of youth in Pensilvania."

The "Advertisement to the Reader" set forth that some gentlemen of public spirit were about to form a plan for educating youth, and called on all who had advice to give as to the parts of learning that should be taught, the order in which they should be taught, or the method of teaching, to send it without loss of time to B. Franklin, printer. The house for the academy, the hints suggested, should be on a spot high and dry, and hard by the bank of a river. Without should be gardens and orchards, meadows and fields. Within should be maps of every land, globes, mathematical instruments, prints, and drawing of buildings and machines. The scholars were to eat together, plainly, temperately, and frugally; were to wear a livery of some sort, that their behavior might the better be seen ; were to be taught to write a fair hand swiftly, and to learn some-

thing of arithmetic, of accounts, of drawing, of
the first principles of geometry and astronomy,
and of the first principles of perspective. To
better their English, they were to read Tillotson
and Addison and Pope, Algernon Sidney, and
Cato's Letters.

Could he have had his own way, neither
Latin nor Greek would have had a place in the
scheme. But the men to whom he looked for
support insisted that they should, and with an
ill grace he put them in. Not a grammar, however, was to be touched till the lads had been
made eager to study the classics. To make
them eager they were to be told that Latin and
Greek were the most expressive, the most co-
pious, the most beautiful of languages ; that
the finest writings, the most correct compositions, the most perfect productions of wit and
wisdom, were in Latin and Greek ; that to render them in English was impossible ; that these
languages contained all science ; that Latin was
the language of the learned in all lands, and
that to understand it was a distinguishing orna-
ment.

This was the great principle that underlay
his plan ; nothing should be taught till the
scholars were impatient to learn it. There
should be no logic till by debating they began
to feel the need of logic. There should be no

mechanics taught till the story of the marvelous machines used in the arts, in manufactures,
in war, had aroused a desire to know something
of the mechanical principles by which such
wonders were accomplished. There should be
no oratory till the study of history had filled
them with admiration of the great things done
by the masters of oratory. There should be no
geography till a knowledge of past events awak-
ened a longing to know the bounds, the situa-
tions, the exact extent of the countries wherein
such events had taken place.

Such in brief were Franklin's proposals.
Those who read them, highly approved. Advice and money were freely given, twenty-four
subscribers agreed to act as trustees, and the
academy was opened January 7, 1750–51, in the
building where it was intended Mr. Whitefield
should preach. The day was a great one. Mr.
Peters preached the sermon ; and when the sermon appeared in print,[1] a new pamphlet by
Franklin was sewed in with it. This was called
" Idea of an English School, sketch'd out for
the consideration of the Trustees of the Phila-

[1] *A Sermon on Education.* Wherein Some Account is given
of the Academy Established in the City of Philadelphia.
Preach'd at the Opening thereof, on the Seventh Day of January, 1750–51. By the Reverend Mr. Richard Peters. Philadelphia : Printed and sold by B. Franklin and D. Hall, at the
Post Office. MDCCLI.

delphia Academy." The "Idea" was merely
the "Proposals" in a new form.

Nourished by subscriptions, lotteries, and
gifts, the Academy and Charitable School of
the Province of Pennsylvania flourished greatly,
became in time the Philadelphia College, and
then the University of Pennsylvania. But the
"Idea" of Franklin was never followed. Year
by year the Latin School was fostered; year
by year the English school languished, till it
fell so far into decay that the trustees endeav-
ored to abolish it. But the charter would not
allow them, and the school dragged on a
wretched existence. Against this stupid attachment to the classics Franklin protested, a
few months before his death, in a pamphlet
called "Observations Relative to the Intentions of the Original Founders of the Academy
in Philadelphia."

While seeking money and founders for the
academy, Franklin renewed his study of electricity. Joined with him in this study was a
man to whose memory posterity has been most
unkind. No one knew how to improve a hint
better than Franklin, and more than one discovery, for which credit has been given to him
alone, came to him in the shape of a very broad
hint from Ebenezer Kinnersley. That Franklin willfully hid the work of his friend there is

no proof whatever. But there is proof that to Kinnersley has never been given anything like due praise, while to Franklin has been allotted much more than is his just share.

To get time to spend in the study of electricity, he sold the newspaper, the almanac, and the printing-house to David Hall, for eighteen thousand pounds, Pennsylvania money, payable in eighteen annual installments of a thousand pounds each. Small as the yearly payment may seem, it was in truth a great one, was about half the profits of the business, was equal to the salary of a provincial governor, and would enable the possessor to live in a style that could not now be kept up on seven thousand dollars. Till the eighteen years had passed, a partnership was to exist under the firm name of Franklin & Hall, and some help was to be given by Franklin in editing the " Pennsylvania Gazette " and writing " Poor Richard." The places which he held under the crown and the colony brought him perhaps one hundred and fifty pounds more.

Thus, at the age of forty-two, this English candle-maker's son, by a strict adherence to the maxims of " Poor Richard," had acquired riches, had retired from business, and had begun that series of remarkable discoveries which, before he was fifty, made his name familiar to

every learned society and to every educated
man in Europe. "I have," he wrote in September, 1748, " removed to a more quiet part of
the town, where I am settling my old accounts,
and soon hope to be quite master of my own
time, and no longer, as the song has it, at every
one's call but my own. If health continue, I
hope to be able in another year to visit the most
distant friend I have, without inconvenience.
With the same view, I have refused engaging
further in public affairs. The share I had in
the late association having given me a little
present run of popularity, there was a pretty
general intention of choosing me a representative of the city at the next election of assem-
blymen ; but I have desired all my friends who
spoke to me about it to discourage it, declaring
that I should not serve if chosen. Thus you
see I am in a fair way of having no other tasks
than such as I shall like to give myself, and of
enjoying what I look upon as a great happiness,
— leisure to read, study, make experiments, and
converse at large with such ingenious and
worthy men as are pleased to honor me with
their friendship or acquaintance." . . .

The fruit of this leisure was rich indeed.
Leaving the electrical apparatus he bought
from Dr. Spence, and the yet finer apparatus
sent over to the library by the proprietary, Mr.

Penn, he turned to the study of the electrical phenomena of nature, with the most marvelous results. Early in 1749 came his " Observations and Suppositions towards forming a new Hypothesis for explaining the several Phenomena of Thunder-gusts." In 1750 he wrote " Opinions and Conjectures concerning the Properties and Effects of the Electrical Matter, and the Means of Preserving Buildings, Ships, &c., from Lightning, arising from Experiments and Observations made at Philadelphia, 1749." Of all his writings on the subject of electricity his greatest is this, for in it is that short paragraph in which he describes and suggests the many uses of the lightning-rod. It had long been a custom with Franklin to make known the results of his experiments in electricity to his old friend Peter Collinson, of London, and by Collinson the letters were from time to time laid before the Royal Society. There they met with that reception which in all ages and by the great mass of all people has always been given to whatever is new. Franklin was laughed at, and the contents of his letters declared to be of no account. But Collinson thought otherwise, and when the " Observations " and " Opinions " reached him, determined that they should be given to the world. `Dr. Fothergill gladly wrote the preface. Cave, of the Gentlemen's Magazine, consented to publish them, and in May, 1751, a little pamphlet entitled " New Experiments and Observations in Electricity, made at Philadelphia, in America," came out and went the round of Europe.   One copy was presented to the Royal Society, and Sir William Watson requested to make an abstract.   A second passed over to France, fell into the hands of the Count de Buffon, was translated at his request by M. Dubourg, had a great sale at Paris, and soon appeared in German, Latin, and Italian.   Louis had every experiment described in the pamphlet repeated in his presence.   Abbé Nollet, who taught the royal children what was then called " natural philosophy," added his mite by asserting that no such person as Franklin existed.   Buffon, De Lor, and Dalibard hastened to put up the apparatus described in the pamphlet for drawing electricity from the clouds, and each succeeded.   Dalibard was first, and on the 10th of May, 1752, demonstrated that lightning and electricity are the same.   One month later, Franklin flew his famous kite at Philadelphia and proved the fact himself.   The Royal Society of London, which had laughed at his theory of lightning, now made him a member, and the next year honored him with a Copley medal.

While the whole scientific world was thus

doing him honor, he suddenly abandoned his studies and went back to politics, and was once more loaded with offices of every sort. His townsmen elected him assemblyman, and he took his seat in 1752. The home government appointed him, with William Hunter of Virginia, postmaster-general for the colonies. The assembly sent him with its speaker to hold a conference with the Indians at Carlisle. There, as he beheld the drunken orgies round the bonfire on the public square, he seems for the first time to have realized the squalid misery to which contact with the white man was fast reducing the Indian tribes. The fruit of his mission was a treaty, and in time a pamphlet, which he named " Remarks concerning the Savages of North America." A tradition is extant that it was written many years afterwards, and printed for his own amusement on his private press at Passey; for it was not given to the world till 1784. As a piece of humorous satire, the " Remarks " deserve to be ranked among the best of his writings. So well is it done that no number of perusals will suffice to determine whether the butt of his wit is the white man or the red; the pious Dutchman of Albany who went to church to hear good things on Sunday and defrauded the Indian during the week, or the ignorant savage who despised civilization and believed the church a place where the pale-face learned to be inhospitable and to cheat.

In public life Franklin displayed great executive power mingled with traits which cannot be too strongly condemned. The vicious political doctrine that to the victor belongs the spoils, he adopted in its worst form, and, though he never sought office, he never, in the whole course of his life, failed to use his office for the advancement of men of his own family and his own blood. When he became a member of the assembly, his place of clerk, made vacant by his election, was by his influence given to his son. When he became postmaster-general of the colonies, he at once made his son controller of the post-office, and gave the postmastership of Philadelphia, in turn to the same son, to a relative, and to one of his brothers. When he was postmaster of the United States, his deputy was his son-in-law, Richard Bache. Yet no man ever performed the duties of the place better than Franklin. In his hands the whole system of the post-office underwent a complete change. He straightened the routes; he cut down the postage; he forced the post-riders to hasten their pace; he opened the mail-bags to newspapers by whomsoever printed, and made their carriage a source of revenue to the crown; he established the penny-post in the large towns; and for the first time advertised unclaimed letters in the newspapers. Mails that used to go out but once a week, began under him to go out three times as often. Riders who in the winter used to make the trip from Philadelphia to New York but twice each month, now, in the coldest weather, went over the route once a week. When in a fit of passion the home government deprived him of his place, the American post-office paid the salaries of the postmasters, and yielded a revenue three times as great as then came from the Irish post-office to the crown.

Franklin began the work of reform by visiting every post-office in the country save that at Charleston, and had scarcely returned from his journey when he was sent to Albany on a matter of great concern. The final contest for the supremacy of France or England in America had begun. Looking back on that contest after the lapse of one hundred and thirty years, it is easy to see that it could not in the nature of things have ended otherwise than it did. Both nations began their occupation of America at almost precisely the same time. The first successful English settlement was made at Jamestown in 1607, and the first successful French settlement at Quebec in 1608. But the purpose for which the men of each race had crossed the Atlantic was totally different. The English came to settle; the French came to conquer. While, therefore, the English were building cities, establishing colonies, founding great commonwealths, planting, trading, and building ships, the French were busy exploring, discovering, erecting forts, and seeking furs and proselytes among the Indians of the Northwest. Hindered from coming southward by the animosity of the Iroquois, the French pushed. into the West, and before 1673 Le Caron, a Franciscan, preached Jesus to the savages on the shores of Lake Huron; Brebœuf and Daniel penetrated to the strait of Sault Ste. Marie; Mesnard reached the waters of Lake Superior, paddled in a birch canoe along the southern shore, put up a church at the Bay of St. Theresa, and lost his life among the Sioux; Allouez explored both shores of the lake, and heard from the Indians of the river Mississippi, which Marquette and Joliet explored. Nine years later La Salle sailed down the Mississippi to the Gulf, and called that magnificent valley, through which the river flowed, Louisiana, after Louis XIV. Before the century ended, Biloxi, in Mississippi, was founded, and in 1702 Mobile. In 1718 Law's Mississippi Company founded New Orleans.

Once in possession of the mouth of the river, France laid claim to all the territory the Mississippi and its tributaries drained, began to encroach on English domain, and built that famous chain of forts from New Orleans to Quebec. In 1731 a band of Frenchmen entered New York and put up Crown Point. In 1750 the whole north shore of the Bay of Fundy, from Chignecto to the Kennebec, was in French hands. They next came up the valley of the Ohio, and built forts at Niagara, at Presque Isle, and on the river Le Bœuf.

Alarmed and justly alarmed for the safety of her possessions, England now bade the colonies arm for defense. So long as the French remained in Canada, or built their forts to the west of the Alleghany range, she cared but little. But now they had crossed the St. Lawrence and the mountains and had begun advancing steadily to the sea, the king was disposed to command his subjects in America to drive the French invaders from the soil. To do this more speedily, the richest, the most populous of the colonies were invited to send delegates to Albany, there to make a treaty with the Six Nations, and frame a plan of common defense. Rhode Island and Connecticut, Georgia and the Carolinas, received no invitation. Their attendance was to be demanded by their sister

colonies, and this demand Rhode Island and
Connecticut alone obeyed. Of those invited,
Virginia and New Jersey did not attend.

Scarcely had the delegates begun to be chosen,
when the French invaded Pennsylvania, and
led away the surveyors of the English Ohio
Company into captivity. Under the narrative
of the capture of Trent and his men, which
appears in the "Pennsylvania Gazette," is a
cut in type-metal of a snake divided into parts,
and beneath it the words "Join or Die."

Both the design and the cutting were the
work of Franklin. The idea of union had
long been in his mind, and to the conference
which gathered at Albany he brought a carefully drawn plan. The credit of that plan is
commonly given to him. But it ought in justice never to be mentioned without a reference
to the name of Daniel Coxe. Thirty-two years
before, when Franklin was mixing ink and
setting type in the office of the "New England
Courant," Coxe published a tract called "A
Description of the English Province of Caro-
lana," and in the preface of that tract is the
Albany plan. So early as 1722 Coxe foresaw
the French aggression, called on the colonies to
unite to prevent it, and drew up the heads of
a scheme for united action. Coxe proposed a
governor-general appointed by the crown, and

a congress of delegates chosen by the assemblies of the colonies. Franklin proposed the very same thing. Coxe would have each colony send two delegates annually elected. Franklin would have from two to seven delegates triennially elected. By each the governor-general was given a veto. By each the grand council, with consent of the governor-general, was to determine the quotas of men, money, and provisions the colonies should contribute to the common defense. The difference between them is a difference in detail, not in plan. The detail belongs to Franklin. The plan must be ascribed to Coxe.

Excellent as the Albany plan was, the colonies and the home government alike rejected it : no unity of action followed ; and the war, which a little energy, a little unity, would soon have ended, dragged on for nine years.

And now that the colonies could devise no scheme for defending themselves, the king determined to defend them, and entrustéd the task to Edward Braddock. Doomed to meet with a terrible fate, he landed at Alexandria in 1755, marched to Fredericktown, and scoured the country for horses, wagons, and army supplies. No sooner was his arrival in Virginia known, than Franklin was sent by the assembly of Pennsylvania to explain why they still persisted in refusing supplies. He performed the mission with his usual tact and skill, and quit the camp with a contract in his pocket to furnish horses, wagons, drivers, and a pack-train to the army of the king. To persuade the farmers of Lancaster and York to part with their beasts in such a cause was no easy thing. But he knew his men, and in a very carefully worded address so tempted their greed and roused their fear, that in less than a fortnight the teams and wagons set out for the camp at Wills Creek.

For this he was thanked by the assembly and praised by the people, who soon gave him an opportunity to serve them again. In the ruin which overwhelmed the army of Braddock, the whole frontier was left exposed. The expedition against Niagara got no further than Oswego. The expedition against Crown Point stopped at the foot of Lake George. Stirred up by the French, and excited by victory, the Indians hurried eastward, and by November were burning, plundering, scalping, massacring, within eighty miles of Philadelphia. Bethlehem was threatened, Gnadenhutten was laid waste. In Lancaster and Easton, men trembled for their lives. To overawe the governor, the assembly, the Quakers, and compel them to put the province in a state of defense, the

mangled bodies of a family the Indians had
killed were carried about the city in an open
cart, and laid out before the state-house door.
The Quakers had long refused either to fight
themselves, or furnish the means for others to
fight. The governor would approve no tax
levy from which the proprietary estates were
not expressly exempt. The assembly would
pass no tax-bill in which the lands of the proprietaries were not included. But, in the terrible days that followed the news of Braddock's defeat, all parties began to give way.
The Penns bade their treasurer add five thousand pounds to any sum the assembly raised
for purposes of defense. The assembly voted
sixty thousand pounds, named Franklin one
of seven commissioners for expending it, and
hurried through a militia bill which Franklin prepared. The preamble exempted Quakers from bearing arms. Numbers of men
would not in consequence enlist. They would
not, they said, fight for men who would not fight
for them. To shame them, Franklin again
had recourse to his pen, and wrote " A Dialogue
between X, Y and Z concerning the present
State of Affairs in Pennsylvania," and published it in the " Gazette."

The effect of the " Dialogue " seems to have
been considerable, and when, in the middle of

December, a call was made for troops to defend
the frontier, five hundred and forty men re-
sponded. Franklin accepted the command, and,
with his son William as aid-de-camp, set out
for the ruins of Gnadenhutten. There he passed
two months hunting Indians and building forts,
till urgent letters came from his friends and
from the governor begging him to return. The
assembly was soon to meet. The old quarrel
was to be renewed, and Franklin could not be
spared.

But the assembly met, adjourned, and met
again, and a new governor came out from England before the crisis was reached. It was in
December, 1756, that the patience of the assembly, so long and sorely tried, gave way.
The affairs of the colonies were desperate. The
French had taken Oswego and Fort George
and razed them to the ground. The expedition
against Ticonderoga had come to naught. That
up the Kennebec had done no better. Fort
Duquesne had not surrendered, while the fort
and settlement at Grenville had been sacked.
The whole frontier of Pennsylvania, indeed,
was unprotected. Meantime the treasury was
empty, and the foe more bold and insolent than
ever. To meet the needs of the hour, the assembly now laid a tax of £60,000, and to make
it acceptable to the governor laid it, not on

the Penn estate, but on wine, rum, brandy, and liquors. But the governor would not consent. A conference followed, the bill came back to the house, and with it came the tart assurance that he would send his reasons to the king.

Then the assembly for the first time began to act and to speak boldly. They ordered such a money bill to be prepared as the governor would sign. They resolved to send home a remonstrance setting forth the evils that would come on Pennsylvania if governed, not by the laws and charters, but by the instructions of the Penns, and they chose two members to represent the province in England. Isaac Norris refused to serve. But Franklin accepted, and the next five years of his life were spent in England.

CHAPTER VI.

1756-1764.

THESE five years were in many respects the
most glorious and the most important in English history. At last the long series of disasters
which had overwhelmed the royal armies had
ended. Since the day the Great Commoner took
the post of secretary, victory had followed victory with amazing rapidity. In July, 1758,
Louisburg surrendered; then Cape Breton
fell; and the great French fleet, the terror of
the coast, was annihilated. Scarcely had the
captured standards been hung in St. Paul's
when 1759 opened, and the nation heard with
delight of the conquest of Goree; of the fall
of Guadaloupe, Ticonderoga, and Niagara; of
the capture of Quebec. Before 1760 closed
Montreal capitulated; the arms of England
were triumphant in Canada, in India, on the
sea, and the old king died.

With the accession of the new king arose a
cry for peace. The Tories, with George III. at
their head, were clamorous for peace on any

terms. The Whigs, with Pitt at their head, were for a vigorous prosecution of the war; and no Pittite believed more firmly in this policy than Franklin, and believing in it he wrote in its defense.

He pretended that, while ransacking the old book-stalls, he had found a book printed at London in 1629. The cover was gone; the title-page was wanting. But he believed the work was written by a Jesuit, and addressed to some king of Spain. Reading it over, he was struck to see how aptly the remarks in one of the chapters applied to present affairs. It was the thirty-fourth, and bore the heading, " On the Meanes of disposing the Enemie to Peace." War, the Jesuit said, with whatsoever prudence carried on, did not always succeed. The best designs were often overthrown by famine, pestilence, and storm; so that enemies at first weak became by these helps strong, made conquests, and, puffed with success, refused to make peace but on their own harsh terms. Yet it was possible by dexterous management to get back all that had been lost by the cross accidents of war. If the minds of the enemy could only be changed, they would often give up, willingly and for nothing, more than could be obtained by force. Now this change of mind, particularly in England, might be secured by the distribution of a few doubloons. There were many men of learning, ingenious speakers and able writers, who, despite their ability, were pinched by fortune and of low estate. A little money would gain them, and, once gained, let them be bidden, in sermons, speeches, poems, songs, and essays, to enlarge mightily on the blessings of peace. Let them dwell on the horrors of war, on the waste of blood and treasure, on commerce destroyed, on ships captured, on taxes greatly increased, on the smallness and sickliness of the captured places, and on the great cost to the country if they be not given back. Let this be done, and the simple, undiscerning many will be quickly carried away by the plausible arguments. Then will rich men having property to be taxed, merchants having ships to lose, officers of the army and navy who wish to enjoy their pay in quiet, unite in one great cry for peace. Then will peace be made, and places lost to the enemy by the accidents of war be willingly restored.

The letter attracted much attention at the time, and found its way into the Gentlemen's Magazine. But the king's friends carried the day and the French and Indian war ended. France was indeed defeated, but she was not conquered. To hold everything taken from her was therefore impossible, and the question became, What shall be given up? Shall it be Canada or Guadaloupe? Shall it be the conquest in America or the conquest in the Indies? The Earl of Bath, in a " Letter to Two Great Men on the Prospect of Peace," was for keeping Canada. William Burke, in his " Remarks on the Letter addressed to Two Great Men," was for keeping Guadaloupe. The author of " The Interest of Great Britain considered with regard to her Colonies " supported the Earl of Bath. Who was the author remained long in doubt. Benjamin Mecom at once reprinted the pamphlet, and ascribed it to Franklin. Franklin during his lifetime was heard to say that in writing it he had been greatly helped by a friend. There is now no doubt that this friend was Richard Jackson, the agent of Pennsylvania and Connecticut in England, that he did most of the work and that Franklin made most of the suggestions. Indeed, it now appears from the manuscripts at Washington that in 1780 a correspondence took place on the subject between Dr. Priestley, Baron Meseres, and the editor of an unknown magazine. The letters of Priestley are gone; but those of Meseres and the editor are preserved, and in them the particular paragraphs Franklin wrote are marked out. Meseres, who had his information from Jackson, ascribes to Franklin all the notes and less than one third the text. He declares also that the lines printed in italics at the heads of the paragraphs ought not to be there, but in the margin as notes.

The pamphlet went through two editions at London and two at Boston, and called forth a long reply. But the answer availed nothing. The Treaty of Paris was signed, and Canada was not given up.

Franklin in the mean while went back to Philadelphia. There for a time he seems to have thought of quitting politics, living at his ease, building a fine house, and passing his time in studying electricity and writing a work on the " Art of Virtue." Had he done so, the book would, unquestionably, have been very ingenious and very amusing, would have abounded in apt illustrations, sound maxims, wit, and good stories well told; but it would have done as little for the encouragement of virtue as the three books of Seneca have done for the suppression of anger.

From such a fate he was happily saved by being again drawn into politics. The rejoicing that followed the Peace of Paris had not had time to die away when the country heard with horror of that great Indian uprising known to history as the Conspiracy of Pontiac. Scarcely had the trees put forth their

leaves when hordes of savages stole from their
villages and laid waste the frontier posts. In
quick succession fell Sandusky and St. Joseph,
and the Miamis forts, and Niagara and Ve-
nango, and Michilimackinac and Presque Isle.
Pontiac himself besieged Detroit. The people
of Le Bœuf quit their village and fled for
their lives. The Indians, sweeping eastward,
attacked Fort Pitt. Scalping parties raided the
whole western border of Pennsylvania, burning,
sacking, murdering everywhere. Thousands
of settlers, leaving everything behind them, fled
to Carlisle. Hundreds more sought safety in
the woods that lined the Susquehanna. The
whole state was in commotion, but nowhere was
the alarm greater than among the Scotch-Irish
of Lancaster. Scattered among them here and
there were little bands of red men the Moravian missionaries had persuaded to accept the
name of Christ. Some were at Bethlehem;
some were at Nazareth; some had been
assigned lands on the Manor of Conestoga.
There, under the influence of the missionaries
they became the most harmless and innocent
of men; put off paint and feathers; put on
hats and clothes, adopted English habits, English names, English speech, and learned to
make, for a living, baskets and brooms. But
to the Scotch-Irishmen of Lancaster they were

still Indians, and Indians were in their eyes
men cursed of God. They were the Canaan-
ites of the New World. The command laid on
Joshua of old was binding still. It was the
duty of every follower of the crucified Lord to
drive out heathen from the land. Threats were
made, sermons were preached, handbills were
spread about, till what was elsewhere a war of
defense became in Lancaster a religious cru-
sade. Alarmed at what was going on about
them, the Indians at Bethlehem and Nazareth
cried out for protection, were taken to an island
in the Delaware, and sent thence under military
escort to the borders of New York. But the
Conestoga Indians, numbering twenty — men,
women, and children, all told — had stayed on
the Manor, and it was on them that, one night
late in December, 1763, a band of fanatics from
Donegal and Paxtang (or Paxton) made a
descent. No more than six of the Indians
were at home, and these were murdered in cold
blood. Horrified at such barbarity, the author-
ities of Lancaster gathered the remnant of the
tribe in the workhouse. Even there they were
not safe, and a hundred brutes from Paxton
and Donegal broke open the workhouse, massa-
cred the fourteen Indians there confined, and
rode away, declaring their next attack would be
on the Indians at Province Island. Nor was the

threat an idle one. Early in January the men of Lebanon, Paxton, and Hanover began forming companies preparatory to the attack.

The Indians, in terror for their lives, begged hard that they might be sent to England. To grant this request was impossible; so it was determined to send them to Sir William Johnson in Central New York. Some Highlanders about to march to New York agreed to escort the Indians. Governor Franklin gave them leave to cross New Jersey, and they were soon safe at Amboy. There trouble arose. Colden would not suffer them to enter New York; they could not stay in New Jersey, and were quickly marched back to Philadelphia, protected by troops sent by General Gage.

At Philadelphia the Indians were lodged in the new barracks in Northern Liberties. Scarcely was this accomplished when news arrived that the Paxton Boys were surely coming. One, Robert Fulton by name, deposed to Penn that he had heard the leading men of Lancaster declare that in ten days' time they would have the scalp of every Moravian Indian in the town. Penn therefore ordered some troops at Carlisle to march into Lancaster, and sent word to the barracks to fire on any body of men that approached in a hostile manner.

On Saturday, the 4th of February, it was

known that the Paxtons were really armed and marching. Some said they were five hundred, some seven hundred, some fifteen hundred strong. What to do, the governor knew not; so he fled to Franklin's house for protection, and summoned the citizens to meet at the statehouse in the afternoon. Though the day was cold and stormy, three thousand at least are said to have obeyed the call, and to have enrolled one hundred and fifty men to spend the night under arms at the barracks. There, all was hurry and preparation. Cannon and powder were brought from the state-house; and during Sunday, carpenters were kept hard at work fortifying the gates, and putting up a redoubt in the center of the barracks yard.

Towards evening, rumors were afloat that the Paxtons had been seen. At eleven and at three at night, expresses rode into town with positive assurance that the enemy was near. Instantly the watch was bidden to shout the news in the streets; the church bells were rung, drums were beaten, and, while the women hastened to put candles in the windows to light the streets, the men set off for the barracks. By sunrise six hundred were under arms, and, to the amazement of the community, not an inconsiderable part were young Quakers.

When something like order had been estab-

lished, scouts were sent out to explore each
road, while parties were dispatched to cut the
ropes and secure the boats at the upper and
lower ferries. Suddenly it was remembered
that the boats at the Swedes ferry on the Schuyl-
kill were not secured, and an armed band
went off to sink them. But they were too late.
The Paxton Boys had already crossed and were
even then at Germantown.

The nearness of the foe increased both curiosity and alarm. Some, who had never beheld
a band of frontiersmen in their life, rode off to
Germantown, and on their return described the
Paxtons as a fine set of fellows, dressed in
blanket coats and moccasins, and armed with
knives, tomahawks, and guns. Others were for
marching out, surrounding the men from Lancaster, and taking them prisoners. But cooler
heads prevailed, and a committee, of which
Franklin was one, met the malcontents on
Tuesday morning, remonstrated with them, and
received a written remonstrance in return.

The document had been written by some one
at Philadelphia and contained eight grievances.
It was thought unjust that, while the counties
of Lancaster, Berks, Northampton, Cumberland,
and York sent in all but ten delegates to the
assembly, Philadelphia, Bucks, and Chester
should send twenty-six. It was felt to be a

grievance that a bill should have been introduced that persons accused of killing Indians
on the frontier should be tried, not in the county
where the alleged crime was committed, but in
Chester, Philadelphia, or Bucks. It was insisted
that while the war lasted all Indians should be
sent out of the inhabited districts; that the
wounded on the border should be cared for at
public expense; that rewards should be offered
for Indian scalps; and that Israel Pemberton
should not be allowed to treat with the Indians
and take gifts of wampum like a governor. This
document delivered, the Paxtons were taken to
the barracks, shown the Indians, and asked to
point out the murderers of their friends. They
could recognize but one, and she an old squaw.
Much pacified, they rode back to Lancaster.

While every Presbyterian preacher, every
Episcopalian parson, and not a few of the Society of Friends, lauded the foul deed of the
Paxton Boys as an act acceptable to God, it is
pleasing to find that Franklin had the boldness
to call it what it was. In a pamphlet entitled
"A Narrative of the late Massacre, in Lancaster
County, of a Number of Indians, Friends of the
Province, by Persons Unknown," he labored
hard to bring the people to a true sense of the
enormity of the crime. He told a plain,
straightforward story of the first murder; men-

tioned the names of the slaughtered Indians; described their harmless character; gave a graphic picture of the second murder, and dwelt with deep contempt on the infamy of justifying such acts by pretending they were sanctioned by a just God. He drew from the history of the Greeks, the Turks, the Moors, the Saracens, the African Negroes, the Six Nations, instances of how sacred these people held that right of hospitality the Paxtons had so shamefully violated. He insisted that, even if the Indians were guilty of the offenses charged, they should have been punished by the courts, not butchered.

And now the people and the assembly were torn by factions in which religion and politics were joined. The Presbyterians and the Episcopalians openly approved the massacre, wrote in defense of it, and supported the action of the mob and of John Penn. The Quakers and the anti-proprietary party denounced the massacre, complained of the conduct of Penn in the matter of the supply bill, taxes, and the war, and warmly defended the Moravian Indians. In the assembly the Quakers and their party were in the majority and determined to do what they had long been urged to do, — petition the king to make Pennsylvania a royal colony.

Accordingly, on the 25th of March, a committee, with Franklin at their head, reported a series of resolutions censuring the proprietaries, describing their government as weak, as unable to uphold its authority or maintain internal peace, and praying his majesty to resume the government of the province, after making such compensation to the Penns as was just. The assembly passed the resolutions, adjourned to consult the people, and met again on May 14th.

Each party made ready for the struggle. Not a day was lost, and by the 1st of April the few printers in the city were hard at work on pamphlets, broadsides, and caricatures. In the whole history of the province there had never been in so short a time such a number of pamphlets issued. Before September, one printer had upon his shelves fifteen, each bearing his imprint. The list of titles contains more than twenty. There were "A Brief State of the Province of Pennsylvania," "A True and Impartial State of Pennsylvania," and "The Plain Dealer," in three parts. "An Address to the Freeholders" replied to one number of "The Plain Dealer." The second number of "The Plain Dealer" replied to "Cool Thoughts on the Present Situation of our Public Affairs," and "Cool Thoughts" was the work of Franklin. He wrote it in great haste, dated it April 12, 1764, and sent men about the city with copies to thrust under the doors, or toss through the open windows of dwelling-houses.[1]

Though done hastily, the work is done well. With a coolness and an honesty found in no other tract, he reviews the cause of the dispute; shows that all the proprietary governments, New Jersey, Maryland, Carolina, have suffered in the same way; and refutes a number of objections which he pretends have been made by "a friend in the country."

The voters having been duly consulted, the assembly met on May 14th to find the speaker's table white with petitions in favor of an address to the king. The debate was long; but the two speeches that best set forth the views of each party were made by John Dickinson and Joseph Galloway. Dickinson spoke in behalf of proprietary government. Galloway replied, and was for a government by the king, and carried the day. The address was voted, and the assembly about to bid the speaker sign, when Isaac Norris, who held the chair, asked for time. He had, he reminded his hearers, been a member of the assembly for thirty years, and speaker for nearly fifteen. He could not support the address, and as he must as speaker

[1] *Plain Dealer,* No. 2.

sign it, he hoped he might have time to pre-
pare a statement of his objections. A short
adjournment was made, and when the members reassembled, Norris resigned. He had
been taken politically sick, sent word he was
too ill to attend, and requested that another be
chosen speaker in his stead. The choice fell
on Franklin, who as speaker gladly signed the
petition to the king, and the assembly rose.

The next meeting was not to take place till
October, before which the annual election was
to be held. As a campaign document, Dickinson at once published his speech, with a long
preface by another hand. Thereupon Galloway's speech appeared, with a preface written
by Franklin. Dickinson then protested that
Galloway's speech had never been delivered.
This brought out a broadside from Galloway,
with certificates asserting that the speech had
been delivered, and a scorching review entitled
" The Maybe." The " Maybe " got its name
from the " ifs " and " maybes " with which
Dickinson's pamphlet abounded.

When he wrote the " Preface to a Speech,"
Franklin unquestionably was thoroughly roused.
The good-nature, the playful humor, the modest suggestions of his earlier pieces were abandoned, and for sarcasm, energy, force of argument, the Preface is unsurpassed.

All this activity served to make him a butt for the wit of caricaturists and pamphleteers. In the corner of one of these singular productions he is represented standing in his study, and underneath him are the lines:

> Fight dog, fight bear! you're all my friends:
> By you I shall attain my ends,
> For I can never be content
> Till I have got the government.
> But if from this attempt I fall,
> Then let the Devil take you all!

In a second he holds in his hand a roll inscribed "Resolved ye Prop'r a knave and tyrant. N. C. D. Gov'r do." The preface to Dickinson's oration contained an epitaph for a monument to Penn, made up of fulsome extracts from the votes of the assembly. Franklin in his Preface ridiculed it in a sketch, " in the lapidary style," of the sons of Penn, far from flattering, made up " mostly in the expressions and everywhere in the sense and spirit of the assembly's resolves and messages." For this he was himself made the subject of a lampoon epitaph in the lapidary style. This summary of his false learning, his political trimming, his treachery, his immorality, his thirst for power, forms a pamphlet of nine pages, and ends with the injunction:

Reader, behold this striking Instance of
Human Depravity and Ingratitude ;
An irrefragable Proof
That neither the Capital Services
Of *Friends,*
Nor the attracting Favours of the Fair,
Can fix the Sincerity of a Man,
Devoid of Principles and
Ineffably mean :
Whose Ambition is
POWER,
And whose intention is
TYRANNY.

" The Scribbler " replied to the " Epitaph,"
but was lost in the host of pamphlets which,
under such names as " The Paxtoniade," " The
Squabble," " The Farce," " The Paxton
Raid," " The Cloven Foot Discovered," " King
Wampum," " A Battle, a Battle, a Battle
of Squirt," overwhelmed the anti-proprietary
party with ridicule and abuse. For rancor,
for that bitter hate which springs from religious bigotry, for foulness both of language
and of thought, the pamphlets named cannot
be equalled.

Everyone knew, as October came on, that the
great contest would be in the city. At the head
of the " old ticket " were Franklin and Galloway ; Willing and Bryan headed the " new."
The Dutch Calvinists and the Presbyterians
to a man supported the new ticket, and were

joined by many of the Dutch Lutherans and Church-of-England men. The Moravians and the Quakers supported the old ticket, and drew some of the McClenaghanites to their side. Promptly at nine in the morning of October 1st the poll was opened, but so great was the crowd that midnight was come before a voter could make his way from the end of the line to the polling - place in less than fifteen minutes. Towards three in the morning of the 2d the new-ticket men moved to close the poll; but the old-ticket men would not, for they had in reserve numbers of aged and lame, who could not stand in the crowd. These they now quietly sent off to bring in, and the streets were soon lively with men being hurried along in chairs and litters to the voting-place. The new-ticket men, seeing this, began likewise to exert themselves, sent off horsemen to Germantown, and secured so many voters that the polls did not close till three in the afternoon. It then took till the next day to count off the votes, which were in round numbers 3,900. When this was done, Franklin and Galloway were found to have been defeated. "Franklin," says one who saw the election, "died like a philosopher. But Mr. Galloway agonized in death like a mortal Deist who has no hopes of a future life."

During the election great numbers of squibs, half sheets and quarter sheets, in English and German, were scattered among the crowd. Some were general in their abuse; some were aimed at Dickinson, some at Galloway, while some bore especially on Franklin. One squib put out by the new ticket is in verse, and ridiculed the preface to Galloway's speech and the intentions of the Franklin party:

> Advertisement and not a joke,
> A speech there is which no man spoke;
> This month or next, 'tis yet a doubt;
> But when 'tis made it will come out,
> Midwif'd by Philosophic Paw,
> Tho' mother'd by a Man of Law.
> They strain'd so hard to do it clever,
> One harm'd his Neck bone, one his liver.
> They vow to get eternal fame,
> All things they 'll charge, yet keep the same:
> Thro' rocks and shelves our bark they 'll paddle,
> And fasten George in Will's old saddle;
> Just as they please they 'll make him sit it,
> Unscrubbed, tho' Will, they say, . . . it.

For the first time in fourteen years Franklin now found himself without a seat in the assembly. But his friends in that body were many and stanch, and promptly presented his name as that of the man best fitted to assist Richard Jackson, the provincial agent, in presenting the petition to the king. Dickinson, who led the proprietary ranks, spent all his strength and

eloquence in opposition. He described Franklin as the most hated man in Pennsylvania.
He declared such an appointment would inflame
the resentments and embitter the discontents
of the people. He called attention to the heap
of remonstrances against such action that lay
on the table, and demanded to know why the
assembly should send to represent the colony
the man most obnoxious to the people, a man
who, after fourteen years of service, had just
been turned out of the assembly. But the
house understood that Dickinson was burning
and longing for the place himself, and, by a vote
of nineteen to eleven, chose Franklin an agent
of the province.

Not content with this defeat, the minority
now protested, moved to have the protest spread
upon the minutes, and again saw their motion
voted down. Thereupon they published the
protest in the newspapers, and were answered
by Franklin in a little pamphlet entitled " Remarks on a Protest." Two days later he set
out for London. But scarcely had the ship put
out to sea when " An Answer to Mr. Franklin's
Remarks on a Late Protest " appeared, and his
friend John Hughes took up his cause. Hughes
proposed that, once for all, the charges against
Franklin should be proved true or false, and
offered to give five pounds to the hospital for

each charge proven true, if some man of character would give a like sum to the hospital for each charge shown to be false. But neither Dickinson nor any of his friends replied.

" Thus," wrote Israel Pemberton the libertine, the King Wampum of the caricatures, " thus Benjamin Franklin is again employed in another negotiation. It is alleged by those who have urged it most that his knowledge and interest will do great service to ye colonies by obtaining some alleviation of those inconveniences we are subjected to by some late acts of Parliament, and of prevention of others with which we are threatened. His dependence on ye ministry for ye Posts he and his son hold forbids my expectation of his opposing their measures with much spirit; and some of us, who know his fixed aversion to ye Proprietaries and their governor, are not without apprehensions, if he can recommend himself by an immediate change of it, that he will soon attempt it." ...

CHAPTER VII.

1764–1776.

On the evening of the 10th of December, 1764, Franklin reached London. As one of the agents from Pennsylvania, his duty was to present the petition with all the speed he could. But he found the three colonial agents striving to prevent the introduction of the stamp act, and joined heartily with them.

From the time the colonies were strong enough and rich enough to furnish men and money to the royal cause, such supplies had always been obtained by requisition. The requisition was a circular letter from the Crown to the governors, was transmitted by the governors to the assemblies, made known the wants of the king, bade the assemblies take these wants into serious consideration, and expressed a firm reliance on the prudence, duty, and affection of loyal subjects to vote such sums of money and enlist such bodies of men as the king needed. To this no objection was ever made. The king obtained the money, and the

people raised it by taxes their chosen representatives imposed.

But now, on a sudden, the British ministry
determined to change the plan. Henceforth
parliament was to lay internal taxes; and the
taxes they proposed to lay and did lay, were
fifty-four in number, and comprised the stamp
act. It is commonly believed that this famous
tax was the first of its kind known in America. But this is a mistake, for twice had
stamp taxes been willingly laid and willingly
borne, and, when they expired, as willingly renewed. The first was imposed for one year by
Massachusetts in 1755, and reënacted in 1756.
The other was passed by New York in December, 1756. It ran for one year, was renewed in 1757 for another year, and created
neither discontent nor opposition. Against
stamp duties, New York and Massachusetts
could therefore make no complaint. It was
against stamp duties laid without consent of the
colonies that the four London agents protested
vigorously on the 2d of February, 1765. Grenville admitted them to audience, listened pa-
tiently to the old plea, no taxation without
representation, and dismissed them, as firmly
convinced of the wisdom of his plan as ever.
On the 22d of March parliament passed the
act. In May news of the passage reached Amer-

ica, and it was soon known in Philadelphia that John Hughes, the man who had so stoutly defended the good name of Franklin, was stamp distributer for Pennsylvania.

Shortly after the passage of the act, Grenville sent for the colonial agents, and, through the secretary, invited each to name a proper person to act as stamp-agent in America. They complied, and Franklin named his old friend John Hughes. The conduct of Franklin in this affair exhibits strange ignorance of the temper of his countrymen. That there would be grumblings, complainings, and threatenings he was fully aware. That there would be open defiance and mob violence seems never to have entered his mind. He looked upon the stamp tax as established, and supposing no opposition would be made, he shrewdly determined to secure from it all the benefit he could. To one friend he wrote: " Depend upon it, my good neighbor, I took every step in my power to prevent the passage of the stamp act; nobody could be more concerned in interest than myself to oppose it, sincerely and heartily. But the tide was too strong for us. The nation was provoked by American claims of independence, and all parties joined in resolving by this act to settle the point. We might as well have hindered the sun's setting. That we could

not do. But since 't is down, my friend, and it
may be long before it rises again, let us make
as good a night of it as we can. We may still
light candles. Frugality and Industry will go
a great way towards indemnifying us. Idleness
and Pride tax with a heavier hand than kings
and parliaments. If we can get rid of the
former we may easily bear the latter." Acting on his own advice, he now attempted to
make a good night of it, and sent over a quantity of unstamped paper to his partner, David
Hall, for assurances had been given that the
paper could be stamped in America. Had this
been allowed, the profit to the firm would have
been considerable. But it was not allowed,
and the paper went back to England to be
stamped, at great cost to Franklin.[1]

[1] His letter regarding it bears date August 9th, 1765.
"I receiv'd yours of June 21 and 22. I have wrote my
Mind fully to you in former Letters, relating to the Stamp
Act, so that I have but little to add except what you desire to
know about the 2*f* on Advertisements. It is undoubtedly to
be paid every Time the Advertisement is inserted. As to the
paper sent over, I did it for the best, having at that time
Expectations given me that we might have had it Stamped
there, in which case you would have had great advantage
over the other Printers, since if they were not provided with
such Paper, they must have either printed but a half sheet
Common Demi, or paid for two Stamps on each sheet. The
Plan was afterwards altered notwithstanding all I could
do. . . .

"I would not have you by any means drop the newspaper,

In July, 1765, the Grenville ministry fell
from power. News of the change was brought
to Philadelphia one Sunday in September. The
people could scarcely wait till Monday to express their joy. The stamp act, they felt confident, was doomed; and all of Monday was
passed in bell-ringing, cannonading, building
bonfires, and drinking toasts. Hughes was
burned in effigy, and, for a time, it seemed
likely that his house would be pulled down.
But all this rejoicing was premature. The
new ministers were as determined to tax America as the old, and the stamp act was not repealed. Then came the associations of merchants and tradesmen pledged to encourage
the growth of wool, to eat no lamb, to wear
homespun, to import no goods of English make,
and to have no dealings with any man who did.
Hughes was remonstrated with, threatened,
urged to follow the example of the stamp
agents in other colonies and resign. But he
would not, and was expelled from the Hand-
in-hand fire company, and denounced as the
enemy of America. So high did the feeling
against him run, that, in September, Galloway
wrote to Franklin that " eight hundred of the

as I am sure it will soon recover any present loss, and may be
carried on to advantage if you steadily proceed as I proposed
in former letters."

sober inhabitants assembled quietly at the instance of Mr. Hughes' friends, and were posted
in several parts of the city ready to prevent any
mischief should that be attempted by the mob."
Nor did Franklin escape. Seeing their opportunity, in the excitement of the moment the
leaders of the Dickinson party assured the
people that Franklin was worse than Hughes.
John Hughes was the open and avowed enemy
of his country : but Franklin was an enemy
disguised as a friend. With a commission as
agent of Pennsylvania in his pocket, he had
done his best to have the stamp act passed, and
he had done so lest he should lose his place
in the post-office. The people believed these
charges, and, as Franklin was beyond their
reach, made threats against his property and
his wife. Mrs. Franklin wrote her husband
that for nine days she had been beset by people
to quit her home, and hurry with her daughter
to Burlington ; that "Cousin Davenport" had
come with his gun to defend her ; that she had
sent for her brother ; and that, while the men
turned a room downstairs into a magazine, she
ordered such defense to be made upstairs as a
woman could manage. She was not molested,
and the proprietary party was content with vili-
fying Franklin in pamphlets and coarse prints.
One caricature shows him with the Devil whis-

pering in his ear. From the mouth of Satan come the words, " Thee shall be agent, Ben, for all my dominions ; " while beneath the figures are the lines : —

> " All his designs concenter in himself,
> For building castles and amassing pelf.
> The public 't is his wit to sell for gain,
> Whom private property did ne'er maintain."

From James Biddle came an address to the electors and freeholders of the Province of Pennsylvania, denouncing Franklin and calling on the voters not to send to the assembly men who would help him at London.

Hughes wrote his old friend that a spirit of rebellion was all aflame ; that a strange frenzy had seized the people ; that not a day went over his head but he was called on to resign, and told to his face that he was an enemy of North America. Yet he could not resign under a threat. The people must do some act of violence. And when violence was once afloat he might himself fall a victim. This seemed unlikely, however, for Coxe, stamp collector for New Jersey, having resigned, Hughes in the same letter begs to have his son Hugh put in Coxe's place.

The day on which the stamp act was to go into force was November 1, 1765 ; but it was not till October that the stamped paper began

to arrive at Philadelphia. On Saturday, the
fifth of that month, the ship Royal Charlotte,
bearing the paper for New Jersey, Pennsylvania, and Maryland, was seen coming round
Gloucester Point. Instantly every American
ship at the port ran up a flag to half-mast;
the bells were muffled and tolled, and a new
demand was made on Hughes to resign. He
did finally give something which was construed
to be a written promise not to serve. As the
1st of November approached, the newspapers
were black with inverted column rules, coffins,
death's - heads, and obituary notices. The
" Pennsylvania Journal," a weekly paper, suspended one issue [1] and then went on regularly
as before. The " Gazette," still owned by
Franklin & Hall, did not suspend. On November 7, the day for the first issue of the " Gazette " after the stamp act became law, a half
sheet was published, printed on one side, without any heading, and in its place the words
" No Stamp Paper to be had." The paper for
the next week was likewise without the customary heading and was called " Remarkable Occurrences." Thenceforth the old name was used.
So determined were the people not to pay the
hateful tax that legal documents of every kind
ceased to be drawn, and the public offices were

[1] No. 1196.   November 7, 1765.

closed from November, 1765, till May, 1766. During these six months, every scrap of stamped paper that was heard of was hunted up, carried to the coffee-house, and burned. Now it was a Barbadoes newspaper brought to Philadelphia by the captain of some ship, now a bill of lading, now a Mediterranean pass. Women of fashion had long abandoned spinning and knitting to their house-maids. But they were now taken up and once again became the mode. To be clothed in fabrics of colonial make was a mark of patriotism, and the demand for such fabrics became so great that one man opened a market for home-manufactured goods, while another set up in his house a number of looms and made thread and cotton stockings. It would have been the ruination of any butcher to have displayed on his stall the carcass of a lamb.

The effect of this conduct was speedy. Not a merchant, not a manufacturer in the mother country, engaged in the colonial trade, but found his American orders canceled and his goods left on his hands. Scarce a ship returned from Boston or Philadelphia without English wares for which there was no sale. Then came up from Bristol, from Liverpool, from Manchester, a cry of distress so piercing that parliament was forced to hear it. Parliament met in December, 1765, and for six weeks merchants, manufacturers, traders, ship-captains, officers of the revenue, of the army, men who had lived in America or were connected with America by interest or by commerce, were called before the commons to give testimony at the bar of the committee of the whole house. With them went Franklin, whose examination on the 2d of February has become historic. Twenty days later the repeal of the Stamp Act was carried, as Walpole declares Lord Rockingham boasted, against king, queen, princess dowager, Duke of York, Lord Bute, the Tories, the Scotch, and the opposition.

The part Franklin bore in promoting the repeal did but little towards restoring him to favor. Carried away by joy, his townsmen did indeed drink a toast, on the king's birthday, to "our worthy and faithful agent, Dr. Franklin." They did indeed sing a song of which a stanza was devoted to his praise, and call a barge which graced the procession by his name. But when the October election came round, he was lampooned more savagely than ever. "A tame sort of opposition his was surely," exclaimed one writer, "being made, no doubt, in the following strain: 'My Lords, it does not become me who hold an office by your indulgence to present any remonstrance that may be offensive to you. My constituents have intrusted

such a remonstrance with me against the Stamp
Act. But after all you will do what you please,
and if it is to be passed, I have a friend, one
John Hughes, who is a bold man, and now
fighting my battles. He will be the fittest person to execute this law, however disagreeable to
the people.' This is the plain English of all the
opposition which it has been ever pretended Mr.
Franklin made to the Stamp Act." "Think,"
exclaimed the writer of another address to the
voters, "let me entreat you to think what
opinions our sister colonies must form of that
man and this province should she embrace, with
the most ardent affection, a native of America
who has aimed a poisoned dagger at the breast
of his parent country. Must not all British
America be convinced that the stamp act was
agreeable to us, when they see us advance to a
post of the most important trust that very man
who has most distinguished himself by pleading
for it? Defend it from the charge of employing
and honoring an instrument whose name is now
flying on the wings of contempt, detestation,
and abhorrence from one end of the continent
to the other." The "Pennsylvania Journal"
declared he was chiefly responsible for the
stamp act. He had mentioned it to Braddock
in 1755. He had proposed it to Lord Bute in
1759, and had seen it planned before leaving

England in 1761. His purpose in coming home was to foment dispute with the governor, raise a cry for a change of government, and be sent back to finish his plan. His plan was to have Pennsylvania made a royal colony and himself made royal governor. But the office of governor was to be his reward for planning and sustaining the stamp act. When, therefore, the act passed, in order to have it faithfully executed he named John Hughes distributer for Pennsylvania and Delaware. While, therefore, other colonial agents who were not to get favor from the king were waiting on the ministers, exciting the London merchants, and contriving to have petitions for repeal sent up from all the manufacturing towns, Franklin remained a quiet spectator. When, therefore, the committee of Bristol merchants visited him with their petition in their hand, he was so reserved and uncivil that they left him in disgust. While the pens of other men were busy denouncing the stamp act and defending the American cause, he had not written one line.

That Franklin had done nothing for the good of the cause was false. That he had written nothing was almost true, for he had sent to the press but one short article. During the early months of 1765 the London press had displayed its usual ignorance of colonial affairs, and had

been full of all manner of contradictory statements. At one moment it was said that the
Americans were about to establish manufactories and ruin the mother country; and at the
next, that there was nothing that the Americans could manufacture. Their sheep were
first described as the finest in the world; and
then as few and the poorest in the world.
When a few dozens of such statements had appeared in print, some friend to America ventured to call their makers to account, and was
himself reproved by Franklin in a short piece
which amused the coffee-houses for a month.
Readers who pretended to know, he wrote, objected, that setting up manufactories by the
Americans was not only improbable but impossible; that labor was so dear that iron could not
be worked with profit; that wool was so scarce
that enough could not be had to make each in-
habitant one pair of stockings a year. But no
one surely would be deceived by such groundless objections. Did not every one know that
the very tails of American sheep were so laden
with wool that each had a little wagon on four
little wheels to support and keep it from drag-
ging on the ground? Would the Americans
calk their ships and litter their horses with
wool if it were not plenty and cheap? Could
labor be dear where one English shilling passed

for twenty - five ?   Some incredulous people
might declare the story of three hundred silk
throwsters being engaged at London, in one
week, to go to New York was a fable, and protest there was no silk in America to throw.
But let them know that agents from the Em-
peror of China had been at Boston treating
about the exchange of raw silk for wool to be
carried in Chinese junks through the Straits of
Magellan.   This was certainly as true as the
news from Quebec that the inhabitants of Canada were making ready for a cod and whale
fishery in the Upper Lakes.   Here again ignorant people might object that the Upper Lakes
were bodies of fresh water, and that cod and
whale were fish never caught but in water that
was salt.   But let these people know that cod,
when attacked, fly into any water where they
can be safest; that whales when they have a
mind to eat cod, follow them wherever they
fly ; and that the grand leap of the whale in
the chase up the falls of Niagara is esteemed,
by all who have seen it, as one of the finest
spectacles in nature.

This manner of treating grave matters in a
humorous way is characteristic of Franklin's
best writings ; and he never overwhelmed his
adversaries so completely as when he met their
ignorance, stupidity, and folly with his good-

natured wit. Two contributions to the newspapers in 1773 are cases in point. The crisis
in the quarrel with Great Britain had then
been reached. The long list of infamous acts
summed up in the Declaration of Independence
had almost been completed. The Townshend
revenue act had been laid and in part repealed ; Gage had taken possession of Boston ;
the " Liberty " had been seized ; the " Gaspée "
had been burned ; citizens of Boston had been
shot down in the streets ; legislatures had been
summoned to meet at places unusual, uncomfortable, far from the depositories of public records ; and the tea flung into Boston harbor.
Enraged at the just resistance of the colonies,
the whole Tory press of England put up a
shout for vengeance. The Americans seemed
to have scarcely a friend left, when two short
pieces in defense of them were printed in the
" Public Advertiser." These pieces, as Franklin
declared, were designed to set forth the conduct of England "towards the colonies in a
short, comprehensive, and striking view," and
to make the view more striking were given uncommon titles and drawn up in unusual forms.
To one he gave the name " Rules for reducing
a great empire to a small one." The other
he called " An Edict of the King of Prussia."
The Rules were twenty in number, were ad-

dressed to all ministers charged with the management of domains so extensive as to be troublesome to govern, and prescribed, as the best way of reducing such empires, precisely the line of conduct Great Britain had taken with America.

In the Edict the King of Prussia was made to assume the same attitude towards Great Britain that George III. had assumed toward America. All the world knew, the Edict stated, that the island of Britain was a colony of Prussia; that the first settlements had been made by men drawn out from Germany by Hengist and Horsa, Hella and Uffa, Cerdicus and Ida; that the colony had flourished for ages under Prussian protection, had been defended by Prussia in the late war with France, and had never been emancipated from Prussian control. As descendants of the ancient Germans, they were still subjects of the Prussian crown, and, as dutiful subjects, were bound to help replenish the coffers exhausted in their defense. On them, therefore, were laid every tax, every duty, every commercial restriction, every manufacturing hindrance imposed by Great Britain on her colonies. Englishmen were forbidden to dig iron, to make steel, to put up rolling-mills, to raise wool unless for manure, to make a hat, or to complain when, for the better peopling of the country, thieves, highwaymen, forgers, and murderers, men of every sort who had forfeited their lives in Prussia, were taken from the jails and sent to Great Britain.

The success of the two pieces was immense. The number of the " Advertiser " containing the Edict went off so quickly that not a copy of it could be had the next day in London. The Rules were copied by the " Gentlemen's Magazine," by almost every London newspaper, and finally, some weeks later, were reprinted in the " Public Advertiser " " in compliance with the earnest request of many private persons and some respectable societies."

With these exceptions Franklin wrote nothing from 1765 to 1773 that is worthy of more than notice. Under the signatures F. B., F+ S, and N. W.; Pacificus, Homespun, Benevolus, Daylight, Twilight, New Englander, A Friend to Both Countries, and Frances Lyn, he published twenty-three short pieces on American affairs in the London newspapers. He wrote a preface to the London edition of the " Farmer's Letters," and an answer to the " Report of the Lords Committee of Trade and Plantations on the Walpole Grant "; republished " The Votes and Proceedings, on November 20, 1772, of the freeholders and other inhabitants of the Town of Boston " with a

short preface, and, under the signature of A
Friend to the Poor, showed the folly of a proposed act of parliament for preventing emigra-
tion to America.

In 1767, Franklin in company with his
" steady good friend Sir John Pringle " set out
for France.   They left London in August, rode
post to Dover, and there began that journey so
pleasantly described in the letter to Miss Ste-
venson.   The French minister Durand had
given to Franklin a bundle of letters to " the
Lord knows who."   But he needed them not,
for his fame had long preceded him, and men of
all pursuits made haste to bid him welcome.   To
him came first D'Alibard, who had repeated
his experiments before the king; and then the
members of the little sect of " Economists."

The Economists professed a deep love of
rural economy and agriculture, and met every
Tuesday in a fine salon in the house of the
Marquise de Mirabeau.   There, after an excellent dinner, they would laud the happiness
of a farmer's life, and, in imagination, chop
down whole forests, drain great bogs, and turn
every barren waste of France into a blooming
garden.

Franklin seems to have known them all.
But with two, M. Dupont de Nemours and
M. Jacques Barbeu-Dubourg, he formed a

life-long friendship. Of Dubourg he was especially fond, and when he again visited France
for a few weeks, in 1769, persuaded the Frenchman to take charge of the translation and publication of his works.

Though his letters and essays were well
known and generally read, they were never, till
1769, gathered into the form of a book. But
in that year a one-volume quarto edition of
what were called his Works was issued at London, and quickly went through four small editions. It was this collection that Dubourg con-
sented to translate. To a general reader the
contents must have been of little interest, for
the " Way to Wealth " was not there, nor the
" Advice to a Young Tradesman," nor any of
the moral and political essays that won him
such fame at home. The whole collection was
made up of letters on electricity, physics, and
science in general. The labor of translation
was given to M. Lesquis ; but the labor of
correcting and revising was left with Dubourg.
The language of Franklin was the plainest
English, and seems, at times, to have sorely
puzzled translator and editor alike. Now they
cannot find a term for " orreries," and Dubourg
in a letter to Franklin begs to know if it may
be rendered " cadrans ; " now he does not
know what " jostled " means ; again he is at

، loss for terms to express the meanings of
"surf" and "spray." But at last all difficulty was overcome, and " Œuvres de M. Franklin, Docteur ès loix, traduites de l'anglois sur
la quatrième édition. Par M. Barbeu-Dubourg,
avec des additions nouvelles et des figures en
taille douce," came out at Paris in 1773.

To the contents of the London edition Dubourg added some letters written between 1769
and 1773, and the "Way to Wealth," under
the title " Le Moyen de s'Enricher, Enseigné
clairement dans la Préface d'un Vieil Alma-
nach de Pennsylvanie, intitulé Le Pauvre
Henri à son aise."

While his friends at Paris were reading the
letters translated by Dubourg, his countrymen
in America were reading with far greater interest another collection of letters for which
they were also indebted to Franklin.

One day towards the close of 1772, Franklin
was lamenting to a member of parliament the
harsh treatment of Boston. The quartering of
the troops especially excited him. The measure
he thought would only make matters worse.
In America the people would think it the act
of the English nation, while it was merely a
ministerial expedient. Tumults would follow,
and the English people, misled by what the
newspapers stated, would declare the Ameri-

cans factious and disloyal. The member of
parliament assured him that he was mistaken;
that quartering troops on the citizens of Boston had not been suggested by the ministry,
nor by any man in England; that it was, in
truth, the work of the Bostonians themselves;
promised to make good the statements, and in a
few days left a bundle of letters in Franklin's
hands. The addresses had been carefully removed, but the signatures were there, and he
was assured they had been written to William
Whately, then dead. In life, Whately had been
a member of parliament, secretary to the lords
of the treasury, under-secretary of state, direc-
tor of the royal progress, a creature of George
Grenville, and a receptacle into which was
poured all sort of information that could not
well be sent direct to his master. It was in
this capacity that Whately received the thir-
teen letters brought to Franklin. Six were
from Thomas Hutchinson, a native of Massachusetts, once lieutenant-governor and then governor of the province. Four were from Andrew
Oliver, likewise a native and lieutenant-governor of Massachusetts. The others were from
Robert Auchmuty, Charles Paxton, and Nathaniel Rogers, men of small note.

Hutchinson and Oliver narrated the events at
Boston from June to December, 1768, described

the people as factious and wicked, recommended that the liberties of the province be greatly lessened, that the governor be made independent of the assembly, that a provincial aristocracy be set up, and that the officers who served the crown be "effectually supported."

Franklin asked leave to copy the letters. This was refused ; but leave was given to send them to America, and they were soon on the way to Thomas Cushing, chairman of the committee of correspondence of the Massachusetts assembly. Cushing was charged not to have them copied or put in print, but to keep them a few months, show them to whom he pleased, and send them back to England. By him they were shown to the foremost men of Boston; and given to John Adams, who carried them on his circuit and showed them to the chief men of Massachusetts. When the general court met they were read, with closed doors, to an amazed assembly. The assembly petitioned the king to remove both Hutchinson and Oliver, and the letters at once appeared in print. Copies of the pamphlet went over to England, where the letters were published in the London journals, to the astonishment of the Tory party. How the Americans got them no one knew. The public suspected Thomas Whately, who owned the papers his brother left. Whately suspected

John Temple, once lieutenant-governor of New Hampshire, who had by permission taken from the papers of William Whately letters of his own. A duel followed, in which Ralph Izard and Arthur Lee acted somewhat as seconds. Whately was wounded. The duel became the talk of the town; and a second meeting was threatened, when Franklin, to prevent further mischief, explained. Through the " Public Advertiser" of Christmas Day, 1773, he assured the public that the letters had never at any time been in the hands of Mr. Whately, that they could not therefore have been taken from him by Mr. Temple, and that neither of them was in any way concerned in sending the letters to America, as he alone obtained and sent them to Boston. This he was justified in doing because they were not private letters between friends, but were written on public matters by public men holding public offices, were intended to bring about public measures, and had been handed about among other public men to lead them to favor such measures. Their purpose was to enrage the mother country against her colonies, to widen the breach already existing, and this they had done.

The ministry saw in this confession a fine opportunity and made haste to use it. Thomas Whately was a government banker, and made some money by paying pensions for the crown. He was now forced to bring suit against Franklin for the recovery of the profits said to have been made by the sale of his brother's letters. The petition for the removal of Hutchinson and Oliver had long been lying, forgotten, in the archives of the Lords of Trade. This was at once taken up, and Franklin was soon before the privy council to answer with regard to the same. It was then the usage for the council to meet in one of the rooms of a building which passed by the name of the Cockpit. Around the fire, and down the sides of the long table, had often been gathered many famous men. But it may well be doubted whether the room had ever held a company quite so distinguished as that assembled to hear the agent of the colony of the Massachusetts Bay insulted, browbeaten, maligned, and defamed. In that room had been done many acts shameful alike to the English government and to Englishmen. But none went down to such a depth of infamy as that perpetrated on that day on our illustrious countryman.

An idle story is still passing current that Franklin in time had his revenge, and that, when about to sign the treaty of peace in 1783, he quit the room to put on the very suit he wore when Wedderburn abused him before the privy council. The story is untrue and was disproved, long before Franklin died, by the published statements of one of the secretaries present at the signing.

The petition of Massachusetts was declared to be scandalous and seditious by the privy council, and was not granted. Franklin lost his place in the post-office, and wrote in defense of his behavior a pamphlet called " An Account of the Transactions relating to Governor Hutchinson's Letters." And now parliament passed the Boston Port Bill, the Massachusetts Bill, the Transportation Bill, the Quebec Act. Then came the first continental congress, and the revolution opened in earnest. As the news of each act of resistance came over to London, the position of Franklin grew daily more dangerous and unpleasant. The whole Tory press set upon him. He ought to be put under arrest. He was the fomenter of all the colonial troubles. He was an arch-traitor, an ungrateful wretch. Was ever an unworthy subject, it was asked, so loaded with benefits by a gracious king? Had he not been made a postmaster-general? Had not his son been made a governor? Had he not been offered a rich place in the salt-office for himself? And what return did he make? With the royal commission in his pocket he had incited his country to rebellion and bloodshed. Johnson called him the master of mischief, who taught congress " to put in motion the engine of electricity, and give the great stroke by the name of Boston." At home the Tory governor sought to deprive him of his pay as agent. The press told the people that he had sold his country for places, and they believed it. For a time his work seemed ended. He shunned the court, went no longer to the levees of the ministers, and kept away from the office of Lord Dartmouth. Indeed, he was about to come home, when news that congress was to meet detained him. While he tarried he wrote a few more essays for the " Public Advertiser," helped Arthur Lee in the preparation of his " True state of the proceedings in the parliament of Great Britain and in the province of Massachusetts Bay, relative to the giving and granting the money of the people of that province and of all America, in the house of commons in which they are not represented," and delivered to Lord Dartmouth the famous Declaration of Rights. This done, he set sail on the 21st of March, 1775, for Philadelphia; landed on the 5th of May, heard with amazement of the fight at Concord and Lexington, and was the next day welcomed home in an ode.

He had been abroad ten years and six months,

and, as he looked about him, he could not but notice the many and great changes that had taken place. Old friends were gone. New faces met him on every street. The growth of the city, the spirit, the prosperity of the people, amazed him. But the greatest of all changes was in his own family and in his own home. The house to which he came and which he called his home, though built nine years, he had never seen. Politics were fast estranging his son. His daughter was married. His wife was dead. Her maiden name was Deborah Read. The story of her life is well known to every one who has read the Autobiography; how Franklin first saw her on the memorable Sunday morning when he walked the streets of Philadelphia in search of a place to lay his head; how he courted her; how he deserted her; how he came back from his first trip to London to find her married to another; how her husband in turn deserted her; how, with many misgivings, Franklin then took her to wife, and how she brought home and reared his illegitimate son. By her Franklin had two children: a son who died in infancy, and a daughter who married Richard Bache and became the mother of Benjamin Franklin Bache, the famous editor of the " Aurora," the bitter hater of Washington, and, under Jefferson, the founder of the Democratic-Republican party. This daughter he found presiding over his house; but his stay with her was short. The Continental Congress was soon to meet, and he was on the day after his landing chosen a member with James Wilson and Thomas Willing.

And now the members began to come in fast. On the 9th of May the Charleston packet brought the delegates from South Carolina. May 10th, every citizen that could procure a horse rode out to welcome the delegates from Delaware, Maryland, Virginia, and North Carolina, who came in a body. May 11th, the members from New England, New York, and New Jersey rode into town, and learned that the continental congress had begun its famous session the day before. Of that glorious congress Franklin was a member fourteen months. During that time he was made Postmaster-General of the United States, was on the committees to frame a second petition to the king; to find out the sources of saltpetre; to negotiate with the Indians; to engrave and print the continental money; to consider the resolution of Lord North; to devise a plan for regulating commerce; to obtain supplies of salt and lead; to establish the post-office; and, when Washington assumed command, to draw up a declaration to be issued by the commander of the army. For work of this kind he was wholly unfit, and in place of a grave and dignified document, he produced a paper that began with idle charges and ended with a jest. Congress most happily never saw the draft and soon employed him in a better way, sent him first on a mission to Washington at Cambridge, and then on a mission to Arnold at Quebec; named him, after the disastrous battle on Long Island, one of three congressmen to confer with Lord Howe; and a little later dispatched him to join Arthur Lee and Silas Deane in France.

CHAPTER VIII.

1776–1790.

THE history of the mission of Franklin to the court of France begins on a November morning, 1776, when a stranger, short, lame, and speaking but little English, made his appearance at Philadelphia. He put up at one of the inns, and sent off a message to the congress, of which the substance was that he had something pressing and important to communicate. No heed was given, for he was thought to be of weak mind. But he persisted, and wrote again and again so earnestly, that Jefferson, Jay, and Franklin were appointed to hear what he had to say. They met him in one of the rooms in the Carpenters' Hall, and were told that whatever they wanted, arms, ammunition, money, ships, would gladly be supplied by France. When the committee asked for his name and credentials, the stranger smiled, drew his hand across his throat, said he knew how to take care of his head, bowed himself out, and was never seen again. The committee, nevertheless, were deeply impressed by what they heard, and had no trouble in persuading congress to name a committee to correspond "with friends in Great Britain, Ireland, and other parts of the world." The committee were active, and letters were soon on their way to Professor Dumas at the Hague, to Arthur Lee at London, and to Franklin's old friend Dubourg. Thomas Story was sent to London, Silas Deane was dispatched to France, and M. Penet, a merchant of Nantes, went back home with a contract in his pocket for gunpowder, guns and supplies.

The months now dragged slowly on without a word from any agent. Winter lengthened into spring, the spring gave way to summer, and the summer was spent before a long letter from Dubourg reached Franklin. So full was it of the most comfortable assurances of help from France that congress lost no time in choosing Franklin, Jefferson, and Deane to make a treaty with that power. Jefferson would not serve, and in an evil hour Arthur Lee was chosen in his stead.

The choice was made on the 26th of September. One month later to a day Franklin boarded the Reprisal and sailed for France. The passage was stormy and the sea covered with English cruisers. More than once the

Reprisal was hotly chased. More than once Captain Wickes beat to quarters and made ready to fight. But he reached the coast of France in safety early in December, and dropped anchor in Quiberon Bay not far from the mouth of the Loire. There he was kept by contrary winds for four days, when Franklin, weary with waiting, landed at Auray and went on to Nantes.

At Nantes he was welcomed with every manifestation of delight, and he stayed there eight days. A story is extant that when Lord Stormont, the English minister, heard that Franklin had landed, he threatened to quit France if the American rebel was suffered to put foot in Paris; that to quiet him messengers were actually sent to Nantes to forbid Franklin coming to the capital; that they were sent by one route when it was well known that Franklin would travel by another; and that, being once at Paris, Vergennes protested that the laws of nations and of hospitality would not allow him to send the old man away. But Franklin had no wish to embarrass the ministry, and, after a few days' stay at Paris, withdrew quietly to Passy, where he ever after remained.

His arrival at Nantes, a lieutenant of police assured Vergennes, had " created a great sensation." But his reception at Nantes was cold

and tame compared with that which awaited
him at Paris. Princes and nobles, statesmen
and warriors, women of rank, men of fashion,
philosophers, doctors, men of all sorts, welcomed
him with a welcome such as had never yet
fallen to the lot of man. To his house came
Turgot, now free from the cares of state, and
Vergennes, who still kept his portfolio ; Buffon,
first among naturalists, and Cabanis, first among
physicians; D'Alembert and La Rochefoucauld,
Raynal, Morellet, Mably and Malesherbes, for
the fame of Franklin was great in France.
Philosophers ranked him with Newton and
Leibnitz. Diplomatists studied his answers in
the examination before the commons of England. The people knew him as Bonhomme
Richard. Men of letters pronounced " The
Way to Wealth " " un très-petit livre pour des
grandes choses," and, translated and annotated,
it was used in the schools. Limners spent their
ingenuity in portraying his features. His
face was to be seen on rings, on bracelets, on
the covers of snuff-boxes, on the prints that
hung in the shop-windows. His bust was set
up in the royal library. Medallions of him
appeared at Versailles. If he made a jest, or
said a good thing, the whole of France knew it.
To one who asked him if a statement of Lord
Stormont the English ambassador was true, he

replied, " No, sir, it is not a truth, it is a — Stormont." And immediately a Stormont became
another name for a lie. To another who came
to lament with him over the retreat through
the Jerseys and the misery at Valley Forge,
he replied, " Ça ira, Ça ira ; " (it will all come
right in the end.) Frenchmen took up the
words, remembered them, and in a time yet
more terrible made them a revolutionary cry.

To the people he was the personification of
the rights of man. It was seldom that he
entered Paris. But when he did so, his dress,
his wigless head, his spectacles, his walking
stick, and his great fur cap marked him out
as the American. If he went on foot, a crowd
was sure to follow at his heels. If he entered
the theatre, a court of justice, a public resort of
any kind, the people were sure to burst forth
into shouts of applause. Their hats, coats,
canes, snuff-boxes, were all à la Franklin. To
sit at table with him was an honor greatly
sought. Poets wrote him wretched sonnets.
Noble dames addressed him in detestable verse.
Women crowned his head with flowers. Grave
Academicians shouted with ecstasy to see him
give Voltaire a kiss. No house was quite in
fashion that did not have a Franklin portrait
over the chimney-piece, a Franklin stove in one
of the chambers, and in the garden, a liberty

tree planted by his hand. The "Gazette" of Amiens undertook to prove that his ancestors had been French.

With adulation so gross were mingled, however, some sneers of contempt. The author of a "History of a French Louse" loaded him with abuse, and described him as a vulgar fellow with wrinkled forehead and warty face, with teeth that might have been taken for cloves had they not been fast in a heavy jaw, and with the manners and gestures of a fop. Marquise de Crequi could not abide him because he ate eggs with pepper, salt, and butter in a goblet, and cut his melon with a knife. " 'Tis the fashion nowadays," sneered a third, " to have an engraving of Franklin over one's mantelpiece, as it was formerly to have a jumping-jack."[1] Capefigue long afterwards described him as one of the great charlatans of the eighteenth century.

But these sneers, if heard at all, passed unheeded. Franklin was an American, and whatever was American was right. One French sheet pronounced the revolution the most interesting of its day. Another printed translations of the circular letters of congress. A

[1] For many facts relating to Franklin in France I am indebted to a most excellent book, "America and France," by Lewis Rosenthal.

third went to the cost of getting news direct
from Boston. All over France the press
abounded with spicy " Anecdotes Américaines."
American maps, books, almanacs were eagerly
sought for. It was now that Suard translated
Robertson's America, that Dubuisson put forth
" Abrégé de la Révolution de l'Amérique An-
glaise," that school-children for the first time
read " Science du Bonhomme Richard."

Seizing the opportunity, Franklin had a
hasty translation of the state constitutions
made by M. Dubourg, and spread them over the
country. The effect was astonishing. Liberty,
constitutions, rights of man, began to be heard
on every hand. Some found fault with the
constitutions of New Jersey and North Carolina for excluding Roman Catholics from office.
Some thought Massachusetts wrong in giving
Harvard College power to bestow honorary
degrees, which were undemocratic. A few
blamed the states for servilely following the
laws and usages of England. But the " Mercure de France " was loud in its praises of the
constitutions, and the opinion of the " Mercure "
was the opinion of France.

There was, however, one point to which
enthusiasm for America did not go. Frenchmen were ready to burst into raptures over the
Declaration of Independence, to laud the thir-

teen constitutions as a "code that marks an
epoch in the history of philosophy," to name
Americans "the brave generous children of
liberty," to call Franklin the Solon and Washington the Fabius of the age, and to hurry
to their maps to put their fingers on Bunker
Hill, on Trenton, and the line of retreat through
New Jersey; they were eager to have their
king send ships and troops and money to the
"insurgents," — but they were not disposed to
invest their private savings in American scrip.

To persuade them to part with their money,
Franklin now wrote "A Comparison of Great
Britain and America as to credit in 1777;" "A
Catechism relative to the English National
Debt;" and "A Dialogue between Britain,
France, Spain, Holland, Saxony, and America,"
had the pieces translated into four languages,
and sent to the money centers of Europe. But
they did not bring forth one groat. Nor can
any one who will take the pains to read them
be at a loss to know why. The style is excellent; the wit is good; the illustrations are
apt; the facts are true. But there is not in
them a single reason which could persuade a
capitalist to loan money to the rebellious subjects of King George. It was true that industry, frugality, honesty, prompt payment of former loans, ought to do much towards settling

up the credit of a nation. It was true that
America had shown all these essentials. It was
true that England owed one hundred and ninety-
five millions of pound sterling; that to count
out so vast a sum in shilling-pieces would take
a man one hundred and forty-eight years; that
when counted the shillings would weigh sixty-
two millions of pounds, and fill thirty-one thousand carts. But it was also true that New
York was in British hands, that the American
Fabius had been badly beaten, that American
independence was yet to be won, and that on
independence hung the value of the American
loan. Poor Richard had himself said, "A bird
in the hand is worth two in the bush," and the
money-lenders took him at his word.

With these exceptions he wrote scarcely anything for months but letters and despatches,
and of them he wrote as few as he could. He
was an old man; he hated the details of business. Moreover, he loved his ease, and was
fond of society, as he found the most brilliant
society in France fond of him. It ceases therefore to be strange that he spent more time in
the company of his companions than in the
company of the suitors and sight-seers that
came to Passy.

John Adams, who joined him a few months
later, drew a sketch of him in a letter to Samuel

Adams, a sketch that is good enough and true enough to be given in the writer's words: " The other you know personally, and that he loves his ease, hates to offend, and seldom gives any opinion till obliged to do it. I know also, and it is necessary that you should be informed, that he is overwhelmed with a correspondence from all quarters, most of them upon trifling subjects and in a more trifling style, with un-meaning visits from multitudes of people, chiefly from the vanity of having it to say that they have seen him. There is another thing which I am obliged to mention. There are so many private families, ladies, and gentlemen that he visits so often, and they are so fond of him, that he cannot well avoid it, — and so much intercourse with Academicians, that all these things together keep his mind in a con-stant state of dissipation." Business might drag, contractors might grow impatient, letters might accumulate, his papers might lie around in hideous disorder. But he must have his after-noon at Moulin Joly, or his evening chat with Morellet at Auteuil. Strangers who came to see him were amazed to behold papers of the greatest importance scattered in the most care-less way over the table and the floor. A few went so far as to remonstrate. They reminded him that spies surrounded him on every hand,

and suggested that half an hour a day given to the business would enable his grandson to put the papers out of the reach of prying eyes. To such his invariable answer was, that he made it a rule never to be engaged in any business that he would not gladly have generally known, and kept his papers as carelessly as before.

The independence of America had not as yet been acknowledged. Nor had the American commissioners, except as private gentlemen, been received by Vergennes. But their business was more than half suspected, and they were soon beset by every man who had anything to gain. To the room which served as an office came merchants seeking for tobacco contracts; soldiers longing for commissions in the army of the United States one grade higher than that which they held in the army of France; contractors eager to supply clothes and ammunition; sea captains begging for letters of marque, and shipbuilders offering vessels of all sizes to be used as privateers. Some came themselves, some brought letters of introduction from strangers of whom the commissioners had never so much as heard. A few wrote. One sturdy beggar sent word to the commissioners, that if they would pay his gaming debts, he would pray earnestly for the success of their

cause. So endless were the demands, and so
various were the forms in which they were
made, that Franklin declared he never met a
great lady, nor was introduced to a man of
rank, never accepted an invitation to dinner,
nor opened a letter, nor heard a carriage roll
into his courtyard, but he felt sure he was to
be pestered for a contract or a place.

To such annoyances were soon added troubles
of a very different sort. The privateers began
to violate the neutrality of France. Lambert
Wickes was thrice ordered from the ports of
France, and twice in open defiance of the command returned. Silas Deane and William
Hodge had fitted out a lugger at Dunkirk and
had given it to Gustavus Conyngham to command, with strict injunctions to capture the
Harwich packet plying between Holland and
England. So well did he obey the commands
that he was soon back in Dunkirk harbor with
" The Prince of Orange " as his prize. The
whole of England was instantly in commotion.
The stocks fell. Insurance rose. The merchants put their goods on board of French vessels, and the English minister complained bit-
terly to Vergennes.

The offense of Wickes was made the subject
of a long letter to the commission on their duty
concerning the neutrality of France. But the

offense of Conyngham could not be winked at;
his prize was taken from him, and he himself
was flung into jail. Nothing daunted, Deane
and Hodge bought and armed a swift cutter,
and applied to the French minister for Conyngham's release. Vergennes was assured that the
vessel should sail at once for the United States.
But Conyngham was scarcely out of sight of
land when he began to make prizes of every
English ship that came in his way, and even
threatened to burn Lynn. Vergennes now
made another show of harshness and for a time
Mr. Hodge was in the Bastille.

The day for such severity was soon to end.
Nothing could check the growing popularity of
the American rebels. Vergennes forbade the
crowds in the coffee-houses to discuss " *des in-
surgens;* " but the people called him a fool, a
dolt, a tool of England, and the discussions went
on. Vergennes objected to the publication of
Dubourg's translations of the State constitutions. The government would not give a license; but the book came out. Letters and
Mémoires, songs and catches, the caricatures,
the nicknames, the street phrases, all bear witness to the popularity of the American cause.
Lafayette joined the rebels, and the nobility of
France was thrown into excitement. The Hes-
sians were captured at Trenton, and all Paris

rushed for maps of America that they might follow the line of the retreat through the Jerseys, and locate the scene of the yet more famous victory. Burgoyne surrendered at Saratoga, and the joy at Paris could not have been greater had the victory been won by France. "When shall we arm in favor of the rebels?" was asked on every hand. The king was forced to answer, "At once." News of the surrender was brought to Vergennes on December 4, 1777. December 16, the commissioners were told the king would recognize the independence of America and make a treaty of alliance at once. February 6, 1778, the treaty was made. In March, Franklin, wigless, swordless, in buckleless shoes and the plainest clothes, made his way with Deane and Lee through a crowd of fops and painted beauties to the dressing-room of the king, to be formally received as a commissioner from America. April 13, 1778, D'Estaing sailed with his fleet from Toulon.

In the flagship with D'Estaing went Silas Deane. Congress had recalled him and in his place sent John Adams, who landed at Bordeaux the very day the fleet left Toulon. There he was received with every manifestation of delight: saw the city lit up in his honor, was visited by innumerable men of note, read with amusement in the "Courier d'Avignon" that he was brother to Samuel Adams, and went on to Passy to add one more to the little company of wrangling Americans. That little band was then made up of Ralph Izard, minister to the Duke of Tuscany, who would not receive him; of William Lee, envoy to the courts of Vienna and Berlin; William Carmichael, once secretary to Silas Deane; Benjamin Franklin, and Arthur Lee. Neither of the Lees could abide Franklin. Franklin in turn detested Ralph Izard; while Arthur Lee never wearied of abusing Deane.

From these disputes Adams wisely kept aloof, turned himself into a drudging clerk, brought order into the office of the commissioners, and joined with all in urging Congress to abolish the commission and make one man minister to France. Congress for once took the advice, re-called Izard, passed over Arthur Lee and Adams, and chose Franklin to be minister to France. Lafayette brought out the commission, and with it came a letter bidding the agents in Europe quarrel no more. But the command was not heeded, and to the last hour of their stay in France, Arthur Lee and Izard lost no opportunity to thwart and annoy Franklin.

After the alliance time became more plentiful with Franklin, and he once more began to write. To this he was prompted by a wish to amuse two fine women, Madame Helvetius and Madame Brillon, whose company he greatly enjoyed. Madame Brillon was the wife of a man of wealth, and the mother of two daughters who played and sang. She dwelt not far from Passy, and to her home Franklin went twice each week to play chess, to hear the music, and sup tea which it was the fashion for the young women to serve. Madame Helvetius dwelt at Auteuil. She was a widow of ample means; for her husband, though a man of letters, had been a farmer-general of France, and to her Franklin seems to have been bound by more than common friendship. Indeed, there are not wanting some to say that, had the lady been willing, he would gladly have made her his wife. To know something concerning her would therefore be of interest; but we are forced to be content with two portraits drawn the one by a man of the world, the other by a woman of New England. In the first, Madame Helvetius is presented to us by Franklin as a woman blessed with many and various friends. Statesmen and philosophers, poets and historians, learned men of every sort, were drawn around her, not because of likeness of taste, for she affected none of their sciences; not because she took pains to engage them, for artless simplicity was a part of her nature; but

because of a charming benevolence, an amiable
desire to oblige, and a disposition to please
and to be pleased they could not find in one
another.

To the wife of John Adams, however, Madame Helvetius seemed a very different creature. Mrs. Adams had joined her husband at
Passy, and had gone with him, one Sunday
evening, to dine with Franklin. As the assembled company sat waiting for the Doctor,
the French woman suddenly entered the room,
and is thus described in a letter by Mrs.
Adams : —

"She entered the room with a careless, jaunty
air. Upon seeing ladies who were strangers to her,
she bawled out : 'Ah, mon Dieu! where is Franklin?
Why did you not tell me there were ladies here?
How I look!' she said, taking hold of a chemise made
of tiffany, which she had on over a blue lutestring,
and which looked as much upon the decay as her
beauty, for she was once a handsome woman. Her
hair was frizzled ; over it she had a small straw hat,
with a dirty gauze half-handkerchief round it, and
a bit of dirtier gauze scarf thrown over her shoulders. She ran out of the room. When she returned
the Doctor entered at one door, she at the other ;
upon which she ran forward to him, caught him by
the hand : 'Hélas, Franklin!' then gave him a double
kiss, one upon each cheek, and another upon his forehead. When we went into the room to dine, she

was placed between the Doctor and Mr. Adams.
She carried on the chief of the conversation at dinner, frequently locking her hand into the Doctor's,
and sometimes spreading her arms upon the backs of
both gentlemen's chairs, then throwing her arm carelessly upon the Doctor's neck. . . . I own I was
highly disgusted, and never wish for an acquaintance
with any ladies of this cast. After dinner she threw
herself upon a settee, where she showed more than
her feet. She had a little lap-dog, who was, next to
the Doctor, her favorite. This she kissed, and when
he wet the floor she wiped it up with her chemise.
This is one of the Doctor's most intimate friends,
with whom he dines once every week, and she with
him."

It is not unlikely that each portrait is in
part correct, and that neither is complete; for
Franklin saw only her mental qualities, and
Mrs. Adams her fashionable follies.

To the weekly gatherings at Auteuil came
Abbé Raynal, and Cabanis, and Morellet, and
Abbé de la Roche, and Franklin, bringing with
him now and then one of his grandsons. Of
what took place on these occasions Franklin
has made no mention, but the Abbé Morellet
has, in his " Memoirs," left us a long account.
From this it should seem that each guest was
expected to contribute to the pleasure of all;
that the meetings were always gay, and that

for songs, anecdotes, good stories, and pieces of wit, the company were never in want. Franklin's contribution was sometimes an apologue, and sometimes one of the "Bagatelles," which he would read or pass round for the amusement of the company. Thus were written, for the abbés and doctors that came to the drawing-room at Auteuil, the "Visit to the Elysian Fields," the drinking-song, and the little piece on the motto, "Truth is in wine." Each of these is good. But the choice bits of humor he reserved for the chess parties and supper parties at Moulin Joli. For Madame Brillon were composed "The Story of the Whistle," "The Ephemera," "The Petition of the Left Hand to those who have the superintendence of Education," "The Handsome and Deformed Leg," "The Morals of Chess," and the famous "Dialogue between Franklin and the Gout." They need no comment. Every schoolboy knows "The Story of the Whistle." Ninety years ago Noah Webster put it in his school-reader, and few school-readers have been without it since. Every chess-player has read "The Morals." Every teacher ought to be converted by the wisdom of "The Petition of the Left Hand." That children are still taught to use the right hand to the exclusion of the left, is a piece of folly of which every educator should

be ashamed. "The Ephemera" is an old piece
in a new form, and is of interest for that very
reason. In 1735 Franklin published in the
Gazette a short essay on "Human Vanity."[1]
The venerable Ephemera there gives utterance
to almost the same lamentation as in the later
piece. But the difference between the two in
language, in arrangement, in wit, is precisely
the difference between Franklin's manner of
writing in his old age and in his youth.

In all editions of Franklin's works in which
the "Bagatelles" are contained, there appears
among them a piece entitled "The Humble
Petitions presented to Madame Helvetius by
her Cats." But it has no business in the collection. Not a line is Franklin's work. Long
after he was dead and gone, his grandson found
among his papers a portfolio marked "Bagatelles." In the portfolio was the "Humble Petition," and when the papers were published, the
"Petition" took its place among them.

The Mémoires of Abbé Morellet, however,
now make it certain that the Abbé was the
author; that he wrote it as late as 1787; and
that he sent it in a letter to Franklin, after the
Doctor had come home to America for the last
time, "as a companion piece," says Morellet,
"to the 'Thanks' you returned for the flies in

[1] *Pennsylvania Gazette*, December 4, 1735.

your rooms, after the destruction of the spiders ordered by Our Lady." What became of the "Thanks" is not known. No trace of the piece exists, even among the papers at Washington. No mention is made of it by any one save Morellet. Such an utter disappearance is strange, for the most trifling of his productions were greatly admired by his French friends, were handed about for perusal, and copied over and over again. They were, moreover, as the manuscripts at Washington show, produced with much pains and labor, and, when written, were looked after with fatherly care. Not a few, indeed, were put in type and struck off on a press set up for his amusement at Passy. The press he bought; but the type were cast in his own house from matrices made by his grandson, Benjamin Bache.

One of the "Bagatelles" so printed is still preserved, and passes by the name "Numb. 705. Supplement to the Boston Independent Chronicle, March, 1782." It is printed in the form in which newspaper supplements were then issued, and contains two fictitious letters. One is from John Paul Jones to Sir Joseph Yorke, defending himself against the charge of piracy. The other is called "Extract of a Letter from Captain Gerrish, of the New England Militia." The captain states that in an expedition to the

Oswegatchie, on the St. Lawrence, a quantity
of peltry was taken, and among it eight pack-
ages of scalps. With the scalps was a letter to
the Canadian governor from James Crauford,
a trader, explaining whence they came and
from whom the Indians took them. Neither
of the letters is remarkable for wit, and so
scarce is the Supplement that it seems quite
likely that not a dozen copies were printed.
Yet, scarce as the Supplement is, the pretended
letter of Crauford seems to be known to men
who have never read so much as the table of
contents of the editions of Franklin's works,
and has in our own day been printed as containing historical facts. Indeed, not long since
a Philadelphia newspaper [1] published the letter
in full, with the assurance that it was "found
in the baggage of General Burgoyne after his
surrender to General Gates;" that it "was
probably sent by an Indian runner to Burgoyne, to be forwarded to the governor," and
that Crauford "was probably a resident British agent with the Senecas."

During the remainder of his stay in France
Franklin wrote but little. For a year his time
was taken up with the framing of the prelimi-
nary articles of peace, and the drafting of the

---

[1] "A gift to King George." *Philadelphia Times*, July 3,
1887.

definitive treaty. But in 1784 he gave to the
world his " Remarks concerning the Savages of
North America," and " Information to those
who would remove to America." Fifty years
ago it was customary to ascribe to him a piece
on the American custom of " whitewashing."
Indeed, some editions of his works contain it.
But the piece was written by Francis Hopkinson and may be found in Carey's " American
Museum."

Franklin had now entered his seventy-ninth
year. Old age had laid upon him many in-
firmities, and he longed more earnestly than
ever to be again in America. He had twice
asked to be recalled, once in 1781 and again
in 1782. Congress answered the first request
by making him a member of the peace commission. But of the second, made after the pre-
liminary articles had been signed, no notice
was taken till March, 1785. It was then accepted with great reluctance, and Thomas Jefferson appointed in his stead.

As he was far too feeble to go to Versailles
to take leave, he wrote a farewell letter to the
minister of foreign affairs, and received in return some gracious words and a portrait of the
king set round with diamonds. He had intended to go by water to the sea ; but he was
not able to set out till July, and the Seine was

then too low. The queen, therefore, loaned him her litter, and in this he went by easy stages to Havre. From Havre he crossed to Southampton. Even there honors awaited him. The British government would collect no duty on his goods. His old friend the Bishop of St. Asaph hastened down to bid him Godspeed, and beg him to write more of the Autobiography while on the sea. But he gave the request no heed, and spent the seven weeks on the ship in writing pamphlets. One treated of navigation, of sails and cables, of ships and their make, of the Gulf Stream, of the ways of giving motion to boats, and of the care to be taken by those about to go to sea. Another dealt with the causes and cure of smoky chimneys. The third was an account of a stove for burning pit-coal.

He was still busy with these when, on the 14th of September, the ship made fast to the Market Street wharf. A discharge of cannon announced his arrival. All the church-bells rang out a merry peal, while crowds of his fellow-citizens hurried to the wharf to meet him, and escort him to his home. The next day the general assembly welcomed him and assured him that his deeds would be set down in history to his immortal honor. The faculty of the University of Pennsylvania, the members of the

16

Constitutional Society, the American Philosophical Society, the officers of the militia, the justices of the city, followed suit. The people instantly chose him a member of the council, and the council and the assembly made him president of the commonwealth. In the crowd that saw him, on the day he took the oath of office, preceded by constables and sub-sheriffs, high sheriff and coroners with their wands, judges and marshals and wardens, and collectors of customs and officers of the tonnage, and all the great officers of state, was a young printer from Ireland. His name was Matthew Carey, and he had when a lad of nineteen offended the English government by announcing for publication at Dublin a pamphlet on the immediate repeal of the penal code against Roman Catholics. The government offered a reward for his arrest. His father suppressed the pamphlet and sent his boy to Paris. There for a while he copied despatches for Franklin, came back to Dublin, started a newspaper, and was soon in jail for lampooning the prime minister. When he was out he came over to Philadelphia, where in 1785 Lafayette gave him the means to found "The Pennsylvania Evening Herald and American Monitor." In the columns of that newspaper he now gave an account of what he saw, and addressed Franklin in some fulsome verses less honorable to his head than to his heart.

Franklin was now at the very height of his fame. Every ship brought him letters from the most renowned men Europe could produce. Not a traveler came to America but turned aside to see him. Pamphleteers and book-makers did him reverence in fulsome dedications. Towns were proud to bear his name. The State of Franklin took its appellation from him. No newspaper mentioned him without some grateful remark. He was "the venerable Dr. Franklin," "the revered patriot Dr. Franklin," "our illustrious countryman and friend of man," "the father of American independence." To his house came regularly the Philosophical Society, the Abolition Society, the Society for Political Education.

The purpose of this society seems to have been to discuss theories of government, and to listen to long papers on the evils of banks, on the blessings of paper money, on the best way to restore the ruined commerce of America. More than one of these papers found its way into print, and it is not unlikely that Franklin himself entertained the members by reading to them from time to time the "Retort Courteous," his remarks on "Sending Felons to America," and his likeness of the Anti-federalists to the Jews.

The paper on the Felons is in one of the

Pennsylvania Gazettes for 1786. He observed
that the British public were growing clamorous
on the subject of the debts due their merchants before the war. But there was a debt
of long standing about which nothing was said,
and which might now be paid. Everybody
remembered the time when the mother country,
as a mark of paternal tenderness, emptied her
gaols into America for "the *better* peopling,"
as she termed it, of the colonies. America was
therefore much in debt on that account; and
as Great Britain was eager for a settlement of
old accounts, this was a good one to begin with.
Let every English ship that comes to our shores
be forbidden to land her goods till the master
gave bonds to carry back one felon for every
fifty tons of burden. These remittances could
easily be made, for the felons she had planted
had increased most amazingly.

The "Retort Courteous" also treats of the
debts. The clamor which had so long been
going the rounds of the British press had now
been taken up by the ministry, and the Americans made to understand that the posts along
the frontier would not be given up till the
debts due the British were paid. The justness
of this conduct is coölly and honestly examined
in the "Retort." The substance of the paper
is, that, having brought America, by their own

wicked acts, to the very brink of ruin, they now cry out that old scores are not settled. General Gage takes possession of Boston, shuts the gates, cuts off communication with the country, brings the people to the verge of starvation, and then tells them if they will deliver up their arms they may leave with their families and their goods. The arms are given up, and they are then told that "goods" mean chairs, tables, beds, but not merchandise. Merchant goods he seizes, and the cry at once goes up, "Those Boston people do not pay their debts."

One act of Parliament shuts the port of Boston; another destroys the New England fishery; a British army harries the country, burns Falmouth and Charlestown, Fairfield and New London; and the whole world is told, "Those knavish Americans will not pay us."

The humane Dr. Johnson, in his "Taxation no Tyranny," suggests that the slaves be excited to rise, cut the throats of their masters, and come to the British army. The thing is done, and the planters of Virginia and the Carolinas lose thirty thousand of their laboring people, and are in turn denounced as men who do not pay their debts. War having put a stop to the shipment of tobacco, the crops of several years are piled up in the inspecting warehouses, and in the private stores of the Virginia

planters.   Then comes Arnold, Phillips, and
Cornwallis, and the British troops. The tobacco
is burned, and the British merchants, to whom
it might have been sent in payment of debt,
exclaim, "Those damned Virginians! why don't
they pay their debts?"

The seventh article of the treaty sets forth
that the king's troops in leaving America should
take no negroes with them. Guy Carleton
goes off with several hundred. The treaty
is thus broken almost as soon as made. But
why should England keep a treaty when the
Americans do not pay their debts?

During 1787 he wrote nothing. He was still
president of the Commonwealth of Pennsylvania. He was a delegate to the convention
that framed the Constitution, and the duties of
the two posts left no time for literature. In
1788 he drew a comparison of the conduct of
the ancient Jews and the Anti-federalists in
the United States of America. In 1789 came
a "Plea for improving the Condition of Free
Blacks;" an "Address to the Public from the
Pennsylvania Society for Promoting Abolition
of Slavery;" and "An Account of the Su-
premest Court of Judicature in Pennsylvania,
namely, the Court of the Press."

The press for two years past had been growing most abusive. Men who two years before

had been held up as models of every repub-
lican virtue had, since the Constitution was
framed, been blackened, named rogue or villain,
and fairly dragged in the mire. Washington
had been called by the Anti-federalists a fool by
nature. The same party had described Franklin a fool from old age. To this he replied
good-naturedly in a letter proposing that to
the liberty of the press should be added the
more ancient liberty of the cudgel. In a humorous way he reviewed the power of the court,
the practice of the court, the foundation of its
authority, by whom it was commissioned, and
the checks proper to be set up against the bad
use of its powers. The authority came from
the article in the State Constitution which
established the liberty of the press, something
every Pennsylvanian was ready to die for, but
which very few understood. To him the liberty
of the press seemed like the liberty of the press
felons had in England; that is, the liberty of
being pressed to death or hanged. If, as many
thought, liberty of the press meant the liberty
of abusing each other, he would gladly give up
his share of the liberty of abusing others for the
privilege of not being abused himself. A great
deal had been said of late about the needs of
checks on the powers of the Constitution. For
like reasons it might be well to put a check on

the powers of the court of the press, and his proposition was, leave the liberty of the press untouched, but let the liberty of the cudgel go with it *pari passu.* Then if a writer attacked you, and put his name to the charge, you could go to him just as openly and break his head. Should he take refuge behind the printer, and you knew who he was, you could waylay him some dark night, come up behind and soundly drub him. This might cause breaches of the peace. Then let the legislators take up both liberties, that of the cudgel and that of the press, and by law fix their exact limits.

The Doctor had now become a great sufferer. The gout had long tormented him sorely. For a year past the stone had kept him much in bed, racked with pain, which he took large doses of laudanum to allay. It was during a brief respite from these attacks that he wrote and sent off to the "Federal Gazette" his last piece. Both the style and the matter make it worthy to close so long and so splendid a career.

The house of representatives had, off and on, for a month past, been considering some petitions on slavery. Two came from the yearly meetings of the Quakers, and prayed that the slave trade might be suppressed. One written and signed by Franklin came from the Pennsylvania Abolition Society, and prayed that slavery might be suppressed. The house sent them all to a committee; the committee made a report, and on that report James Jackson, of Georgia, made a violent pro-slavery speech. Franklin read it with just contempt, and turned it into ridicule. He pretended to have read in an old book called " Martin's Account of his Consulship" a very similar speech on a very similar petition. The speaker was Sidi Mehemet Ibrahim, a member of the Divan of Algiers, and the occasion a petition of the sect of Erika or Purists, praying that the practice of enslaving Christians might be stopped. The speech of Ibrahim against granting the prayer is a fine parody of that of Jackson, and worthy of Franklin in his best days.

But his best days were gone. The stone became more painful than ever. Early in April, pleurisy attacked him ; an abscess of the lungs followed, and on the night of April 17, 1790, he passed quietly away. His body, followed by a great crowd of citizens, was laid by that of his wife in the yard of Christ Church. For a time the mourning was general. The newspapers appeared with inverted column rules. Congress wore a black badge for thirty days. But in France the demonstration was greater still. The National Assembly put on mourning. The city of Passy gave his name to a street. He was lauded by Fauchet before the Commune of Paris; by Condorcet before the Académie des Sciences; by Rochefoucauld Liancourt before the Society of '89.

CHAPTER IX.

THE AUTOBIOGRAPHY.

No sooner was the great man dead than his life and works fell a prey to biographers and editors. For this he was himself to blame. Long before he died, he saw many of his letters and pieces published and republished, in magazines and newspapers, both at home and abroad. He well knew that, do what he might, they would live. Yet he would not arrange and publish them himself, nor gather them with a view to being published by his executors. The great discoveries with which his name was joined, the events in which he had borne so striking a part, made his life of no common interest to his countrymen. Yet it was only by pestering that he was led to go on with an Autobiography begun with diffidence, and never brought to a close.

So much as now makes the five opening chapters was written during a visit to the Bishop of St. Asaph, at Twyford, in 1771. The visit over, the writing stopped, and the manuscript was left to begin a career more strange than any in the history of literature.

When Franklin set out for Paris in 1776, he left his papers in the care of his friend Joseph Galloway. Galloway carried the trunk containing them to his home in Bucks County, and placed it in an outhouse that served as an office, turned loyalist, and hurried to the army of Howe at New York. Abandoned thus to the care of his wife, his property fell a prey to the vicissitudes of war. Pennsylvania confiscated the estate. The British raided the house, smashed the trunk, and scattered the papers of Franklin over the floor, where they lay for months. A few were picked up by Benjamin Bache, and in time a bundle of them fell into the hands of Abel James, a Quaker, and an ardent admirer and warm friend of Franklin. James found the packet to consist of a quantity of notes, and twenty sheets of closely written manuscript. It was that part of the Autobiography which had been written at Twyford in 1771. Delighted that such a treasure should have come in his way, James made a careful copy and sent it in 1782 to Franklin at Passy. With it went an urgent letter begging him to go on with so profitable and pleasing a work. The warmth of the appeal, the sight of the fragment long thought lost, were not without

effect upon him. His labor had not been wast-
ed. A purpose once abandoned might yet be
accomplished. He hesitated, sent both letter
and manuscript to his friend B. Vaughan, and
from Vaughan, in 1783, came back a still more
urgent entreaty to go on.

Franklin was then deep in affairs of state.
Peace negotiations were on foot. The treaty
was being framed. He was too busy making
the history of his country to find time to write
the history of his life. But in 1784 he undertook the task, and worked with diligence till he
went home in 1785, when he once more put the
work aside. But his friends would not suffer
him to abandon it. Again and again Benjamin
Vaughan and M. le Veillard besought him to go
on. Again and again he promised and excused
himself. His papers were in disorder. His office
left him no time. He would go on with the
work when the Constitutional Convention rose.
But when it rose he was suffering too much
from the stone. At last, in 1788, the promise
was kept. The Autobiography was brought
down to 1757, and a fair copy sent to Dr. Price
and Benjamin Vaughan. The original went to
M. le Veillard and Rochefoucauld-Liancourt at
Paris. Thus a second time the manuscript
left the author, and a second time was doomed
to a series of strange adventures.

Hardly were the copies safe in Europe when Franklin died. His books and papers passed by will to his grandson, and the work of editing began. With a promptness he never showed again in the whole course of his career, Temple Franklin wrote at once to M. le Veillard, told him of the disposition made of the papers, claimed the manuscript of the Autobiography, asked him to show it to no one unless some eulogist appointed by the Académie, and bade him hold it, sealed in an envelope, addressed to the owner. The letter bears date May 22, 1790. But long before it was read at Passy, the Eighty-nine Society of Paris had listened with delight to a fulsome eulogy of Franklin pronounced by Rochefoucauld. The speaker assured the hearers that Franklin had written his memoirs; that the manuscript was then in France, and that it should be published the moment any additions that might have been made to it came over from America. He has been accused of keeping his word; for in March, 1791, "Memoirs de la vie privée de Benjamin Franklin, êcrits par lui-même, et adressés à son fils. Suivis d'un précis historiques de sa Vie politique, et de plusieurs Pièces relatives à ce Père de la Liberté," came out at Paris. Buisson was the publisher. But who the translator was, how he got the manuscript.

and who owned it, can never be known. He would not, the editor said in the preface, give any account of the way the original manuscript came into his possession. He had it. It was in English. If any critic chose to disbelieve it, let him leave his name with Buisson, bookseller, Rue Hautefeuille No. 20, and when four hundred subscribers were secured the memoirs should be published in English. The manuscript in his possession, it was true, came down no further than 1731. Doubtless the family of Franklin would soon give his memoirs to the world in a more completed form. But the editor was sure the heirs of the great man could never be persuaded to give the history of his early years. Their vanity would not permit it. Should they, as he feared, suppress this first part of the memoirs in their edition, the world at least would be obliged to him for having preserved it.

Scarcely was the book out when M. le Veillard hastened to disavow it. On March 21, 1791, he wrote a long note to the " Journal de Paris." He did not know, he declared, how the translator got his copy. He had no part in the act. What had appeared was not a third of what he had, which came down to 1757.

That Veillard told the truth is not to be doubted. It is to his efforts more than to any

one else that we owe the existence of the Autobiography. He gave Franklin no peace till it
was written, and, having obtained the manuscript, nothing could have induced him to publish it in so bad a form. The Buisson translation is shamefully done. We have " misse
Read" and "mistriss Godfrey," but "M. Den-
ham, M. Grace," and " Rev. M. George White-
Field." Cooper's Creek becomes "Sooper's
Creek," Edinburgh is " Edinbourg," "in the
Grub-street ballad style " is rendered "des
chansons d'aveugles." When compared with
the original manuscript as given in Mr. John
Bigelow's edition, dates are found to be wanting, names suppressed, names of cities inserted,
and whole paragraphs wanting.

While these things were taking place at
Paris, Temple Franklin was gathering his
grandfather's papers at Philadelphia. That
none might escape him, he thrice inserted this
advertisement in his cousin's newspaper :

" DR. FRANKLIN'S PAPERS.

" Towards the end of the year 1776, the late Dr.
Franklin, on his departure for Europe, for greater
security deposited a large chest, containing his papers and manuscripts, with Mr. Joseph Galloway, at
his place in Bucks County, in Pennsylvania. The
same was left there by Mr. Galloway when he

quitted his habitation, and was, it is said, broke open by persons unknown, and many of the papers taken away and dispersed in the neighborhood.

"Several of the most valuable of these papers have since been recovered ; but there are still some missing, among which are a few of the Doctor's Letter Books and a manuscript in four or five volumes folio, on Finance, Commerce, and Manufactures. The subscriber, to whom Dr. Franklin bequeathed all his papers and manuscripts, and who is preparing to give his works to the public, takes this method of informing those who may have knowledge of any of the above mentioned papers, and will communicate the same to him so that he may thereby be enabled to recover any of them, or who may themselves procure any of them and deliver them to him, shall be thankfully and generously rewarded and no questions asked. He likewise requests those persons who may have any letters or other writings of Dr. Franklin that may be deemed worthy the public eye, to be so kind as to forward them as early as possible, that they may be inserted in the Doctor's Works.

"Those, also, who may have any books or maps belonging to the library of the late Dr. Franklin, are desired to return them without delay, to the subscriber, who is about to embark for Europe.

"W. T. FRANKLIN."

What response was made to his call is not known. That some of the letter-books and papers were sent back is quite likely, and with these, towards the close of 1790, Temple Franklin hurried over to London. He was just in time. For no sooner did the Buisson edition come out at Paris than two separate translations were begun at London. By positive assurances that he was about to publish the Autobiography complete, the translations were put off for two years. In 1793 both were placed on the market.

One bears the imprint of J. Parsons, is a literal translation of Buisson's edition, and was done by a man as ignorant of French as the French translator was of English. Franklin called one of his early ballads " The Lighthouse Tragedy." The Frenchman rendered this "La Tragédie du Phare;" and this, in the English copy, is given as " The Tragedy of Pharaoh." What Franklin called a swimming-school becomes a " school of natation." His expression " Grub-street ballad style " is softened into "blind men's ditties." There are the same blanks, the same errors, the same putting-in and leaving-out of words, and the same shortening of paragraphs, as in the French edition. The book most happily was never reprinted.

The reason for this was the issue, at the same time, of a far better translation by Franklin's old friend Richard Price. This was made in 1791. But Price soon followed Franklin to the grave, and to please the grandson the translation was held back. The preface declares that the basis of the work was the Paris edition of 1791. A letter from Price asserts that he has read the Autobiography as far as complete, and the character of the book shows that he had. Now, for the first time, the missing dates are given, the errors corrected, and the English made to resemble the English used by Franklin. But the Autobiography ends at 1731. It is safe, therefore, to believe that Temple Franklin had recalled the copy sent to Mr. Vaughan, and that he would not let Dr. Price see it. Certain it is that the Doctor found himself forced to patch out the life with such fragments of biography as he could get, and that he used for this purpose a sketch by Henry Stuber, of Philadelphia.

Stuber was a young man of great promise. Before he was sixteen he was graduated at the University of Pennsylvania, began the study of medicine, took his degree, and was deep in the study of law when death cut short his career. Nor were his friends the only ones who watched him with interest. The public also expected much from him, for he had issued proposals for publishing a translation of Shoepp's "Travels in America," a work that never has been, but richly deserves to be, translated, and had become a writer for the "Columbian Magazine." His contribution to the Magazine consisted of a Life of Franklin, in the numbers for June, July, September, October, November, 1790, and February, March, May, and June, 1791. The performance is in no wise remarkable, but bears strong evidence that Stuber was suffered to at least read over the copy of the Autobiography in Temple Franklin's keeping. Many of the statements in the Life can be accounted for in no other way.

Up to this time only so much of the Autobiography had been made public as Franklin wrote at Twyford in 1771. But in 1798 a new edition was issued at Paris, with much of the second part composed in 1784 at Passy. Even this encroachment on his literary property could not make Temple Franklin bestir himself. Indeed, twenty years were yet to go by before he would make good his promise. Meantime book-makers, reviewers, and newspaper critics, weary of delay, began to abuse him. To these men his conduct was perfectly clear. He had sold himself to the British government.

These charges first take shape in the early part of the present century, in the "National Intelligencer," a Jeffersonian newspaper published in the city of Washington. The editor declared that the public were tired with waiting for the appearance of Dr. Franklin's works; that something was wrong; that a rumor was current that the papers of the great man would never be published; and called on his descendants to explain. No explanation was made, and in 1804 the "National Intelligencer" repeated the charge. Silence, he declared, had given the subject increased weight. More than eight years before, Benjamin Franklin Bache had often declared that an edition was surely coming out at the same time in Europe and America. Why had it not come? Some said because Mr. Temple Franklin had sold his copyright to Dilby, a London bookseller, who in turn had sold it for a greater sum to the British government, in order that the papers might be suppressed.

The effect of this was to bring out the Duane edition. Duane was owner of the "Aurora," and husband to the widow of Benjamin Franklin Bache, and had thus come into possession of a number of books and papers Temple Franklin had not secured. These he determined to publish, and in 1805 announced in the "Aurora" that subscriptions would be received for a three-volume edition of Dr. Franklin's works. The publication began in 1808, and went on till 1818, when, instead of three, six volumes had been issued.

The charge of fraud, once started, crossed the Atlantic, and next appears in 1806 in the preface to a three-volume edition of Franklin's works, edited by Benjamin Vaughan at London. Vaughan declares, that when Temple Franklin thought his labor done, he offered the manuscript to the London printers, but that his terms were high, that the printers demurred, and that nothing more was heard of the offer. "The reason was plain. The proprietor, it seems, had found a bidder of a different description in some emissary of government, whose object was to withhold the manuscripts from the world, not to benefit it by their publication, and they either passed into other hands, or the person to whom they were bequeathed received a remuneration for suppressing them." The preface is dated April 7, 1806. The charge which it contains was sifted, denied, and pronounced foolish by the "Edinburg Review" for the July following. But it had meanwhile recrossed the Atlantic, and in September, 1806, appeared in the "American Citizen," a newspaper published by James Cheetham at New York.

"William Temple Franklin," says the writer, "without shame and without remorse, mean and mercenary, has sold the sacred *deposit* committed to his care by Dr. Franklin to the

British government. Franklin's works are lost
to the world forever." And now the charge
went over to France, and was taken up by
"The Argus, or London Review," a journal
published at Paris, March 28, 1807. To this,
Temple Franklin had the folly to reply. The
editor had the courtesy to declare the reply a
full and satisfactory answer to the slander,
and the matter stood just where it did in the
beginning. Men went on asserting and believing it, and it was as late as 1829 printed, with
a vast deal more of similar nonsense, in Jefferson's "Anas."

The truth seems to be this: Temple Franklin did the best he could, and the best he could
do was worthless. He was fussy, he was slow,
he was cursed with the dreadful curse of putting off. What the duty of an editor was, he
never knew. His time was squandered in sort-
ing, arranging and rearranging, reducing here,
adding on there, cutting a piece from one place
to paste it on at another, till the manuscript
was a mixture of paper, paste, and pins; till
the work was neither his own nor his grandfather's.

When he could stand it no longer, Colburn,
the publisher, persuaded Temple Franklin to
have a clerk, and sent him as such a man who
knew something of editing. Then the labor

went on more rapidly till a new trouble arose. Colburn would risk but six volumes. There was manuscript enough to make ten, and Franklin insisted that all should be printed. It was finally settled that six should be issued, should be looked on as the first installment, and if all went well the rest should follow. Thus in 1817, twenty-seven years after Temple began his labors, the first genuine edition of his grandfather's writings came forth from the press. The six octavo volumes were issued from 1817 to 1819. But a three-volume quarto edition appeared in 1818.

And now the used and the unused papers were cast into an old chest, and left in the vaults of the banking house of Herries, Farquhar & Co., St. James Street, London, while Franklin went over to Paris. There he lived, married, and died. His wife, as executrix, administered on his estate, and on September 23, 1823, took the trunk from the vaults of the banker, and for seventeen years the Franklin manuscripts again were lost to history. Colburn seemed to care nothing about them. Sparks was unable to find them. Nor were they found till 1840, when they were discovered done up in loose bundles on the top shelf of a tailor-shop in St. James. The shop was in the building where Temple Franklin had lodged. The finder was once a fellow-lodger, and by right of discovery now claimed them as his own. Too lazy to read them, he supposed them merely the originals of what was already in print, and offered them, as such, to the British Museum, to Lord Palmerston, to a long succession of American ministers to England. But nobody wanted them till Abbott Lawrence sent him to Mr. Henry Stevens, who bought them in 1851.

Their true character then came out. Many indeed had been printed. But among them were the letter-books and manuscripts once believed to be lost. By Mr. Stevens they were sorted, repaired, arranged; the pins were taken out; the pasted pieces were soaked apart, the manuscripts restored to the state in which Benjamin Franklin left them, and, bound in Bedford's best manner, they were in 1882 sold to the United States government for $35,000.

To describe the collection is impossible. In it are the Craven Street letter-book; the Hartley correspondence; the letters concerning the Hutchinson Papers; the records of the American legation at Paris; the correspondence of the commissioners to negotiate for peace; and the original manuscripts of the essays, squibs, and bagatelles. There, too, in the original, is the famous letter to Strahan; the petition of the Congress of 1774 to the King; Franklin's

"Articles of Belief and Acts of Religion;" and two bagatelles on "Perfumes," and "Choice of a Mistress," which are unhappily too indecent to print. The manuscript of the Autobiography is not there.

The tradition runs that when M. le Veillard lost his head during the Reign of Terror, the copy given to him by Doctor Franklin passed to his widow; that Temple Franklin asked it from her, that she demurred, and that he gave her in exchange the original sheets in his possession. Madame le Veillard gave them in turn to her daughter, who bequeathed them to her cousin, who left them to her grandson, who made them over in 1867 to Mr. John Bigelow, then minister from the United States to France. Mr. Bigelow at once put out a new edition of the Autobiography, and the world knew for the first time that what it had for fifty years been reading as the Life of Franklin was garbled and incomplete. Temple Franklin traded manuscripts with Madame le Veillard that he might get a clean copy for the printer. But when the clean copy which he published is compared with the unclean copy which he gave away, they are found to be very different. More than twelve hundred separate and distinct changes, says Mr. Bigelow, have been made in the text. The last eight pages of the manuscript were not printed.

As to the nature of these changes little need be said. They are usually Temple Franklin's Latin words for Benjamin Franklin's Anglo-Saxon. They remind us of the language of those finished writers for the press who can never call a fire anything but a conflagration, nor a crowd anything but a vast concourse, and who dare not use the same word twice on the same page. Thus it is that in the Temple Franklin edition "notion" has become "pretence," that "night coming on" has become "night approaching," that "a very large one" has become "a considerable one," that "treated me" has become "received me"; that "got a naughty girl with child" has become "had an intrigue with a girl of bad character"; that "very oddly" has been turned into "a very extraordinary manner." But the changes did not stop here. The coarseness of the grandfather was very shocking to the grandson, and "guzzlers of beer" is made "drinkers of beer," "footed it to London" becomes "walked to London," "Keimer stared like a pig poisoned" is made to give way to "Keimer stared with astonishment."

Such changes are perhaps of small account, yet they cannot be read without a feeling of contempt for the man who made them, and a feeling of thankfulness to the man who pointed

them out.   That an editor should use judgment
in the choice of what he publishes, is true ; but
that he should have the face to change one word
of the text made public, is something that cannot be too strongly denounced.   Mr. Stevens
maintains that Franklin wrote every one of them
with his own hand.   It is out of the question.
It is impossible to believe that Franklin, who
formed his style by a study of the Spectator,
ever hesitated to use plain English.   Nor would
Mr. Stevens have believed it had he been owner
of the Le Veillard manuscript.

Whoever, therefore, would read the Autobiography as it was written must go to the Bigelow edition.   There, too, is kept the original
spelling.   The work richly deserves a reading.
Since the day whereon it was first made public,
innumerable books written by our countrymen
have come into fashion and gone out of fashion
and all but disappeared.   Hardly a man whose
name adorns the American literature of the first
half of the century but saw his books pass
through a period of neglect.   Irving did, and
Cooper, and Halleck, and Willis, and Hawthorne, and many more.   But the Autobiography of Franklin has suffered no neglect.   With
the great mass of our people it has always been
popular, and has in the United States alone
been republished fifty-one times.   What is bet-

ter, the people read it. Such records as can
be had from public libraries all over the
country reveal the fact that the book is
read at each of them on an average of once
a month. At some, where the humblest and
least educated come, its popularity is amazing. Indeed, at the Cooper Union Library
in New York, the Autobiography, during
1885, was called for more than four hundred
times, and the Life by Mr. Parton upwards of
one thousand. If it be put with books of
its kind, and judged as an autobiography, it
is beyond doubt the very best. If it be treated
as a piece of writing and judged as literature,
it must be pronounced the equal of Robinson
Crusoe, one of the few everlasting books in the
English language.

In the Philadelphia high school, a part of it
is used as a text-book. Save " Poor Richard,"
no other piece of Franklin's is so widely admired, and on these two most unquestionably
rest his literary fame.

Of the pieces which make his collected Works,
there is little to be said. The range of subjects is wonderfully wide. They abound in
hard common sense and wit. The style is delightful, and the language good plain English.
But they were not collected and arranged by
himself, and his fame has suffered accordingly.

No man, unless it be Thomas Carlyle, has ever been so harshly treated by editors and biographers. Acting under the belief that every scrap and line of Franklin's writing ought to be kept, they have been most diligent collectors.

Buisson, Doctor Price, and the compiler of Robinson's edition, published whatever came to hand. Temple Franklin published everything his publisher could be induced to take. Sparks labored hard to let nothing escape him. Editors since Sparks have, in their eagerness, had the face to ascribe to Franklin pieces Francis Hopkinson is well known to have written. The result is a collection of "Essays," "Notions," "Remarks," "Thoughts," "Observations," "Letters," no human being will now read unless forced to, which he will then consider a sore trial, and which cannot be called by any other name than tiresome. Franklin reads a pamphlet on impressing seamen, and jots down along the margin a few remarks in pencil. They were never intended to be put in print. They were never intended to be seen by any one save himself. They were perhaps the crude thoughts of the moment, and may, for all the reader knows, have never recurred to him again. But his editor spies them, and thrusts them into his collected writings. Yet not one of them is more apt, or more profound, or more sagacious, than could be made by any well-educated lad of twenty. Some notions on trade and merchants, some thoughts on the Sugar Islands, some reflections on coin, are found among his papers, or are communicated in a letter to a friend. Not one of them is more remarkable than may be heard any day in a street-car, or read any morning on the editorial page of a newspaper. Yet these too are given a place in the collected writings.

With all this diligence, however, the editors have suffered some of his best pieces to escape them. No one has gathered the Dogood Papers, nor the sketches written for the Courant, nor the essays in the Pennsylvania Gazette, nor the Prefaces and Prognostications of Poor Richard. Mr. Parton and Mr. Bigelow alone have reprinted Polly Baker's Speech. It is to be hoped that some day, not far in the future, this will be corrected, and that to the fifty editions of his works in English will be added one more containing such of his writings as give him a place in the goodly company of American men of letters. Out of such a collection will be left the notes which he jotted down on the margins of his pamphlets; the books and pamphlets he distinctly declares he did not write; all his pieces on political economy; everything written to affect public opinion, and which, to be understood, must now be annotated and explained. In that collection will surely be found the Speech of Miss Polly Baker before a Court of Judicature in New England; The Witch Trial at Mount Holly; Advice to a Young Tradesman; Father Abraham's Speech; Remarks concerning the Savages of North America; the Dialogue with the Gout; The Ephemera; the Petition of the Left Hand; the pretended chapter from Martin's Account of his Consulship; a few of the best essays from the Gazette; the prefaces from the Almanac; the Parables; the Whistle, and the Autobiography.

And yet, when this is done, the place to be allotted Franklin among American men of letters is hard to determine. He founded no school of literature. He gave no impetus to letters. He put his name to no great work of history, of poetry, of fiction. Till after his day, no such thing as American literature existed. To place him, with respect to Irving, Bryant, Cooper, Prescott, and the host of great men that came after him, is impossible. There is no common ground of comparison. Unlike them, he never wrote for literary fame. Had he cared for such fame, he would not have

permitted friends and strangers to gather and
edit his writings during his lifetime; he would
not have suffered death to overtake him when
the Autobiography was but half done; he
would not have made it an invariable rule
to never send anything to the press over his
own name. His place is among that giant
race of pamphleteers and essayists most of
whom went before, but a few of whom came
immediately after, the war for independence.
And among them he is easily first. Their
merit lies in what they said: the merit of
Franklin lies not only in what he said, but in
the way in which he said it.

In his youth he was an imitator of Addison,
and of all the countless host of imitators he is
nearest the master. His wit is as keen, his
humor is as gentle, his fancy is as light and
playful, his style is sometimes better. Addison
has drawn no characters more lifelike than
Alice Addertongue, and Anthony Afterwit, and
Celia Single, and Patience Teacroft. Richard
Saunders and his wife Bridget, and the " clean
old man," Father Abraham, are as well done as
the " Spectator." To compare any of these, save
" Poor Richard," with the short-faced gentleman
and his friend, Sir Roger and Will Wimble,
would be unjust to Franklin. But when they
are compared with Will Serene and Ralph

Simple, and Mary Tuesday and Will Fashion, or any sketched and dismissed in a single paper, it must be allowed that in Franklin the illustrious Englishman has his match.

It should seem, therefore, that the essays of Franklin should be as well known. That they are not is due to the fact that they are so few in number, and that they were never collected till the reading public had begun to outgrow the taste for such writings, and when it would have been hard even for Addison to have made much of a reputation by the "Spectator." That they are so few is to be ascribed to his versatility and his sloth. He could do so many things that to do one thing long was impossible. A pamphlet that could be written in the heat of the moment; a little essay or a bagatelle that could be finished at one sitting, and trimmed and polished at a couple more, was about all he had the patience and the industry to accomplish. He finished nothing. Neither vanity nor persuasion could make him complete the Autobiography. The Dogood Papers he dropped as suddenly as they began. The "Busybody" he abandoned to his friend Breintnal. Then he set up a printing-house, a newspaper, and an almanac, and created Mr. Richard Saunders. But he soon grew weary of "Poor Richard," and dropped him; grew tired of business, and though the printing-house was immensely profitable, sold it that time might be had for the study of electricity. From electricity he was drawn off to politics, and from politics went back to electricity, made discoveries and wrote essays so important that he became world-famous; that the Royal Society elected him to membership; that the University of St. Andrews bestowed on him the title of Doctor, by which he has ever since been known. Success so marked, it should seem, would have kept him faithful to his studies of science. But he was soon again deep in politics, was held there for years by circumstances he could not control, and made for himself so great a name as a diplomatist and politician, that as such he is now chiefly remembered. During these years he still continued to write, and produced a mass of political literature, effective in its day but now forgotten.

These writings have none of the cool reasoning of the "Farmer's Letters"; none of the stirring appeals of "Common Sense" and the "Crisis." Their characteristics are brevity and humor. Grave as the quarrel was, he looked upon it as he looked upon the small bickerings and petty acts of tyranny of neighbors and townsmen, and, as a humorist, held up the folly and injustice of England's behavior to laughter and to scorn. Nothing, perhaps, so finely illustrates this tendency to be at all times the laughing philosopher, as his draught of an address to be put forth by Washington on taking command of the army.

The alliance made and the treaty signed, he once more went back to general essay writing, and to the end of his life continued to produce pieces with the old traits of brevity and wit. If the writings of his youth were Addisonian, those of his old age were thoroughly French. When his mind was racked with the "Spectator," he wrote "Silence Dogood," and the "Busybody," and "Patience Teacroft." When he had lived some years at Passy, he wrote the "Bagatelles." Even among them there is a choice; yet they all have the brightness, the spirit and vivacity, of the best French writing of that day. His last piece, the speech in the "Divan of Algiers," is not surpassed by any of the pleasantries of Arbuthnot or Swift.

Except the Bagatelles, which he wrote in his old age for the amusement of his friends, he produced little which did not serve an immediate and practical purpose, and which was not expressed in the plainest and clearest English. A metaphor, a simile, a figure of speech of any kind, is rarely to be met with. The characteristics of his writings are, short sentences made up of short words, great brevity, great clearness, great force, good-humor, apt stories, pointed allusions, hard common sense, and a wonderful show of knowledge of the practical art of living. Knowledge of life he had in the highest degree. He knew the world; he knew men and the ways of men as few have known them. His remarks on political economy, on general politics, on morality, are often rash and sometimes foolish. But whatever he has said on domestic economy, or thrift, is sound and striking. No other writer has left so many just and original observations on success in life. No other writer has pointed out so clearly the way to obtain the greatest amount of comfort out of life. What Solomon did for the spiritual man that did Franklin for the earthly man. The Book of Proverbs is a collection of receipts for laying up treasure in heaven. "Poor Richard" is a collection of receipts for laying up treasure on earth.

His philosophy was the philosophy of the useful,— the philosophy whose aim it is to increase the power, to ameliorate the condition, to supply the vulgar wants, of mankind. It was for them that he started libraries; that he founded schools and hospitals; that he invented stoves; that he discovered a cure for smoky chimneys; that he put up lightning-rods; that he improved the post-office; that he introduced the basket-willow; that he first made known the merits of plaster-of-paris as a manure; that he wrote " Poor Richard "; that he drew up the Albany Plan of Union.

For this it is now the fashion to reproach him as the teacher of a candle-end-saving philosophy in which morality has no place. The reproach, if it be one, is just. Morality he never taught, and he was not fit to teach it. Nothing in his whole career is more to be lamented than that a man of parts so great should, long after he had passed middle life, continue to write pieces so filthy that no editor has ever had the hardihood to print them. The substance of all he ever wrote is, Be honest, be truthful, be diligent in your calling; not because of the injunctions " Thou shalt not steal, thou shalt not bear false witness against thy neighbor; " but because honesty is the best policy; because in the long run idleness, knavery, wastefulness, lying, and fraud do not pay. Get rich, make money, as a matter of policy, if nothing more, because, as Poor Richard says, it is hard for an empty sack to stand upright.

Low as such a motive may seem from a moral standpoint, it is, from a worldly standpoint, sound and good. Every man whose life the world calls successful has been actuated by it, and Franklin is no exception. What he taught he practiced. His life is a splendid illustration of what may be done by a never-flagging adherence to the maxims of Poor Richard.

The language in which he put his thoughts was plain and vigorous English. This is all the more praiseworthy as most American writers of his day used a vicious Johnsonese. But he spelled English as if it were his, and not the king's. In all his manuscripts, " through " is " thro'," " surf " is " surff," " job " is " jobb," " extreme " is " extream." Sometimes such words as " public," " panic," " music," end with a *k* and sometimes they do not. As might be expected of a man self-educated and so practical, he firmly believed in phonetic spelling, made a system of his own, and invented a quantity of hieroglyphics that look very much like bastard type, to represent his peculiar alphabet. In it he had neither *c*, nor *q*, nor *x*, nor *j*, nor *w*; no letter which did not stand for a distinct sound, and no distinct sound which did not have a letter. To his reformed spelling he made but one convert, and she, by dint of much labor, learned to read it with some fluency and write it with some ease. Towards the end of his days he was himself converted to a like system of Noah Webster.

When we turn from Franklin's labored pieces to his letters, we find that they, too, are worthy of notice. They abound in worldly wisdom, in shrewd observations, in good-humor, good stories, good sense, all set forth in plain English and in an easy, flowing style. In them is displayed to perfection the independence of thought, the sagacity, the direct and simple reasoning, the happy faculty of illustration by homely objects and parallel cases; that invincible self-control which neither obstinacy, nor stupidity, nor duplicity, nor wearisome delay could ever break down; and, what is better than all, the fearless truthfulness so characteristic of the man. Where all are good, to choose is hard. But it is idle to expect that the readers of our time will peruse the stout volumes into which Mr. Sparks has gathered a part of them. It may therefore be well to name a few which may be taken as samples of all, and these few are: the letter on the habits and treatment of the aged; that on early marriages; the account of his journey to Paris; the three on the Wilkes mob in London; the moral algebra; that containing the apologue on the conduct of men toward each other; that on the art of producing pleasant dreams; that on the Cincinnati; that to Mr. Percival on dueling; to his daughter on ex-

travagance; to Mason Weems on the ordina-
tion of American Protestant Episcopal clergy-
men; and that to Samuel Mather. To these
should be added the two letters on how to
do the most good with a little money, because
of the sound advice they contain and the excellent practice they recommend.

To say that his life is the most interesting,
the most uniformly successful, yet lived by any
American, is bold. But it is nevertheless
strictly true. Not the least of the many
glories of our country is the long list of men
who, friendless, half-educated, poor, have, by
the sheer force of their own abilities, raised
themselves from the humblest beginnings to
places of eminence and command. Many of
these have surpassed him. Some have specu-
lated more deeply on finance, have been more
successful as philanthropists, have made greater
discoveries in physics, have written books more
commonly read than his. Yet not one of them
has attained to greatness in so many ways, or
has made so lasting an impression on his countrymen. His face is as well known as the face of
Washington, and, save that of Washington, is
the only one of his time that is now instantly
recognized by the great mass of his countrymen. His maxims are in every man's mouth.
His name is, all over the country, bestowed on

counties and towns, on streets, on societies, on corporations. The stove, the lightning-rod, and the kite, the papers on the gulf stream, and on electricity, give him no mean claims to be considered a man of science. In diplomacy his name is bound up with many of the most famous documents in our history. He drew the Albany Plan of Union. He sent over the Hutchinson Letters. He is the only man who wrote his name alike at the foot of the Declaration of Independence, at the foot of the Treaty of Alliance, at the foot of the Treaty of Peace, and at the foot of the Constitution under which we live. Nor is he less entitled to distinction in the domain of letters, for he has produced two works which of their kind have not yet been surpassed. One is "Father Abraham's Speech to the People at the Auction." The other is "The Autobiography of Benjamin Franklin."

INDEX.

JOHN BACH MCMASTER holds the distinction of having been the first professor in the United States to combine teaching with research and the writing of history. As Professor of History at the University of Pennsylvania from 1883 to 1920, McMaster produced the monumental eight-volume *History of the People of the United States*. Immensely popular, McMaster's *History* assured its author an enthusiastic audience and the respect of his scholarly colleagues. *Benjamin Franklin* sprang in 1887 from the same careful historical technique that made McMaster's larger work so successful.

LARZER ZIFF is Professor of English at the University of Pennsylvania and has been on the faculty of Oxford University and the University of California at Berkeley. Author of *The American 1890s* and *Puritanism in America*, he is currently working on a book examining literature and society in the time of Emerson and Melville.